Never Abandoned

Michelle Yost
& Nicole Yost

TRILOGY CHRISTIAN PUBLISHERS
TUSTIN, CA

Trilogy Christian Publishers
A Wholly Owned Subsidiary of Trinity Broadcasting Network
2442 Michelle Drive
Tustin, CA 92780

Rights Department, 2442 Michelle Drive, Tustin, CA 92780.

Trilogy Christian Publishing/TBN and colophon are trademarks of Trinity Broadcasting Network.

For information about special discounts for bulk purchases, please contact Trilogy Christian Publishing.

Trilogy Disclaimer: The views and content expressed in this book are those of the author and may not necessarily reflect the views and doctrine of Trilogy Christian Publishing or the Trinity Broadcasting Network.

Manufactured in the United States of America

Trilogy Disclaimer: The views and content expressed in this book are those of the author and may not necessarily reflect the views and doctrine of Trilogy Christian Publishing or the Trinity Broadcasting Network.

10 9 8 7 6 5 4 3 2 1

Library of Congress Cataloging-in-Publication Data is available.

ISBN 978-1-63769-758-0

ISBN 978-1-63769-759-7(ebook)

Contents

Introduction v

The Abandoned Train Car 1

The Abandoned Child.. 7

Leaving the Past Behind 18

Feeling Abandoned... 23

Abandoned Character 29

Abandoned Mercy 36

Life and Death 42

Abandoned News... 48

Abandoned Gifts... 53

The Abandoned Room in the Art Museum................. 59

Abandoning the One True God 65

The Final Exam.. 74

The Harvest.. 82

The Stolen 93

Construction Site 102

Unaware 112

The Sacrifice 119

The Plane Ride 123

Faith in the Father 128

The Abandoned Key and Lock Store 135

The Ice Hotel 141

The Class Assignment 144

Those Dirty Words 150

The Wood Shed 155

The World that Serves Self 158

Decision 162

Never Abandoned 166

Abandoned Vengeance 172

Conclusion 176

Citations 180

Introduction

The power of stories on the human heart is undeniable. It is evident by the success of modern media in our culture today. Books, movies, and television shows have found immense success because people can't get enough of stories that move their hearts in some way. Whether it is a drama, comedy, horror, or fantasy, there is a story to be told that resonates strongly with people!

These stories resonate with people so profoundly because in some way, they are relatable. Even if the stories operate in a fantasy world, the trials and successes of the characters are things we can walk with them through and learn from. Think of your favorite book, movie, or TV show. There is likely a character there that has touched your life in some way. Perhaps they have inspired you so much so that it has changed how you see yourself and the world around you. Stories hold that kind of incredible influence.

I have seen people come to faith time and time again through the power of a story. These stories have come from so many different sources. I have seen people come to faith through the personal testimonies of others, through stories from the Bible, or even through fictional stories that have shown them a new perspective on God and the world around them. There is a message to be found in every story, and it could very well change the life of the reader.

Just take a look at the remarkable popularity of the Marvel cinematic universe in the past few years. Multiple entries in this series have become some of the biggest and highest-grossing films of all time. They have an audience of unimaginable proportions and have brought in more revenue than is easy to comprehend. The stories may be over the top and involve many flights of fantasy. Still, they remain so popular and relatable because, at their core, they involve stories of relatable people going through relatable things. They overcome trials in life and give us hope to do the same.

God helps us each write our own story, beginning to end. He is the creator and sustainer of all life. He wants to walk alongside us through life. He is not content ruling over creation from a distance: God wants to be an intimate part of your every day. God is ever-present among us! As we journey through life with Him, He helps us craft each chapter of our story. Because of His influence and the way He works in our lives, our stories hold a beautiful power within themselves as well.

I cannot emphasize enough the importance of sharing our own stories with others. They too have the power to change lives. God has made them that way. He desires that we would move the hearts of others towards Him and His kingdom. We all have a story to tell, and we never know how it will resonate with someone. Just by sharing the journey you have been on, you can potentially change another person's life forever.

God experiences perfect community, unity, and love within Himself as expressed through the Holy Trinity. He created us out of an overflow of that love. That means that we were made to be relational beings, both with God and with others. Part of what makes a relationship powerful is sharing our stories with others. This is our calling as a child of God: to influence others to the faith with our stories and to encourage other believers through the retelling of God's faithfulness in our lives.

We see countless stories throughout God's Word. It often feels like the Bible is much more focused on stories than on rules or teachings. That's because God knows how much we connect with stories! Just look at all of Jesus' teachings, for instance. They were almost entirely taught in parables. There was a reason for that. Those stories stick with us in a way that helps us remember and comprehend them in a way we couldn't if they were told to us in another way.

Look at how the Bible begins in Genesis 1:1: "In the beginning..." It is a narrative. In His Word, God is telling us a story. It's a story about Him, ourselves, and the world He created. It is a story that encompasses the past, present, and future. Through this grand narrative of God, we learn everything we need to know to live faithful lives as His children. Not only that, but His story also gives us incomparable hope for the present and future. God's Word leaves us lacking nothing in life.

A wonderful example of a biblical story that has captured and inspired the hearts of so many is the story of Mary Magdalene. Luke 8:1–2 says,

> Soon afterward Jesus began a tour of the nearby towns and villages, preaching and announcing the Good News about the kingdom of God. He took his twelve disciples with him, along with some women who had been cured of evil spirits and diseases. Among them were Mary Magdalene, from whom he had cast out seven demons. (NLT)

Throughout the gospels, we learn that Mary's life was held back by the demonic influences that plagued her. It had cost her her reputation, healthy relationships, a means to provide for herself, and countless other hardships. These struggles had sent her life out of control. She had come to such a place where she was powerless to do anything to reverse it on her own. She was in desperate need of a Savior.

And that's exactly what she received. Jesus came into her life and brought immense healing. He cast out the demonic influences within her, giving her a renewed sense of identity, purpose, and self-worth. From this point on, we see her many times among the disciples throughout the gospel story. Christian tradition also tells us that she went on to wield incredible influence in the early church and brought salvation in Christ to many souls. Jesus walked alongside her and helped her write her story, and He wants to do the same with you today.

This story of deliverance and overcoming trials has given so many people the power they need to endure and defeat struggles in their own lives. It is the perfect example of how God gives us these accounts to transform our reality. Stories like these make evident the power and the presence of God's Holy Spirit within us. They remind us of God's power, faithfulness, and promises, even during the midst of our trials when they are so hard to see.

God placed it upon my heart to share this collection of short stories in the hopes that it would encourage, inspire, and help you along your spiritual journey. These stories are filled with hope, encouragement, life lessons, and reminders of God's ever-present status in our lives. I pray that these stories meet you in whatever part of your journey you find yourself on at the moment and spurn you forward towards a deeper relationship with God.

I ask that you read these stories with a prayerful and reflective heart. Invoke God's presence into your reading time and ask Him to transform your heart as you pray and read. Make this time of reading time spent together with God. Ask that He would reveal hidden wisdom and insights to you as you are restored in His presence. As you do, God will help you to write your own story according to His powerful purpose for your life.

The Abandoned Train Car

I remember the first time I met Bianca, a contractor in Florida. She was helping my longtime friend of thirty years, Dena, remodel her master bedroom and invited me over to her house to show me some of her exotic animals. Bianca is in her early thirties with long blonde hair, a contagious smile, and a passion for animals that runs in her family. Her parents owned a pet store while she was growing up.

I was greeted at Bianca's front door by her two French bulldogs, one of which being deaf. She was so kind to open her home to me in order to show me a chameleon, a panda iguana, a pink hognose snake, and a leopard gecko. She spent at least an hour-and-a-half with me explaining their feeding habits, where they are from, and so on. She is now interested in adopting a baby macaw to add to her small animal kingdom.

Towards the end of this fascinating educational briefing and handling of these unusual animals, she mentioned an abandoned train car on the outskirts of her enormous acreage. Half a mile due east of her front yard stood an abandoned train car that had been there for generations.

She gave me a quick synopsis of the railroad tracks and abandoned train car: During the mid-1800s, Bianca's family used the railroad to transport their crops to neighboring counties.

With a half-liter of cold water in hand, Bianca led me to the front door and gave me exact directions to the abandoned train car.

The heat was overwhelming as I walked to my destination; sweat was running down my back. A cool front was expected later that night, which would be very welcoming.

After walking forty minutes, I arrived at a rusted train car with all of the windows open to the elements. As I climbed the three steps into the car, I glanced at the graffiti covering the sides and ceiling. Green ivy vines crept through the open windows. I also noticed that the rubber flooring was worn, torn, and curled up in many places. It was littered with empty water bottles, leaves, and tree limbs. There was only one passenger metal seat in the front right of the train car that could accommodate two people. I sat down on the hot metal seat.

I glanced out at the wooded area that surrounded me. I leaned back on the metal seat and closed my eyes to rest for a second before I walked back to Bianca's house.

I fell asleep.

I felt the rhythmic motion of the train as the landscape rolled by me. I was waiting for the conductor to come through to stamp my train ticket. I looked around the empty car; I was in the first car as we were rounding a curve. As I peered out the open window, there were many train cars. I could see a red caboose in the far distance.

Imagine if each train—no matter the number of cars—represented one individual's life. What would each train car carry and represent as we journey through life?

Perhaps, each train car could be "a fruit of the Spirit."

"But the fruit of the Spirit is love, joy, peace, forbearance, kindness, goodness, faithfulness, gentleness, and self-control. Against such things, there is no law" (Gal. 5:22–23).

"God prefers fruits of the spirit over religious nuts."—Adrian Rogers, author and former pastor of Bellevue Baptist Church in Memphis, Tennessee.

As the train rolled down the tracks, suddenly, I found myself in complete darkness as it traveled through a tunnel. It felt like a bullet train. Cool air blew through my hair.

Aren't our lives similar to a bullet train racing full throttle through life? Our calendars are full of activities, with our smartphones alerting us of our next meeting and long to-do lists. The hustle and bustle never stop. We travel through life from our work to family life, to the grocery store, to barbeques with neighbors, college classrooms, sports with the kids, and on it goes. We have become self-absorbed with our careers, money, power, and possessions.

For some of us—our train derails during our life's journey.

We must honestly ask ourselves: *Are we living for God or self?*

In Luke 11:15–32, Jesus tells the parable of the Prodigal Son. This is a story that is familiar to most of us. Consider the prodigal son. Was he living for God or self? He took his share of his father's inheritance and spent it all on wild living. He did what he wanted, when he wanted, not thinking of how he represented his family or used his father's money, but only about his own enjoyment. He wasn't living for God. This way of life eventually brought disaster upon him, sending him crawling back to his father, begging for forgiveness as he realized the corruption in his own heart.

Billy Graham once said, "We do not fail to enjoy the fruit of the Spirit because we live in a sea of corruption; we fail to do so because the sea of corruption is in us."

I could feel the train's movement slow down as we made it through the tunnel. As the train screeched to a halt, I stood up and grabbed the handrail, and stepped down unto the platform. I looked around, and the train conductor was standing off to my left. He waved me over with surprise on his face.

We said our hellos, and I asked, "Why did the train stop?"

The conductor looked at his clipboard in his hand and scanned through pages of paperwork.

"There are four train cars that will be added to this train: Justice, Mercy, Grace, and Share Your Testimony. The layover may be long. We are trying to locate the car called Share Your Testimony," the conductor said with confusion on his face.

"And you, my young lady, should have never been on this train. Right outside this train depot are several taxis," as he glanced back at his clipboard.

"Justice is God giving us what we deserve. Mercy is God not giving us what we deserve. Grace is God giving us what we don't deserve."—Adrian Rogers

"For it is by grace you have been saved, through faith-and this is not from yourselves, it is the gift of God" (Eph. 2:8). There is nothing we can do to earn salvation. Sin has already separated us from God, and there's nothing we can do to overcome it on our own. Thank God for Jesus! He makes it possible to approach God once again. We

mustn't do good works because we think they will bring us salvation: we must do them out of an earnest desire to serve others and the Lord Himself.

I was suddenly awoken by Bianca calling my name and her French bulldogs licking my hand.

"There you are!" Bianca said. "I started to worry. You have been gone for three hours."

Bianca, her French bulldogs, and I were walking back through the woods to her house in silence. My thoughts went back to the train tracks, the train depot, and cars. Throughout life, we can pick up or drop train cars, change lanes, adjust our speed, pick up and drop off people amongst the many depots along our path. But once we reach the end of the railroad tracks, we can no longer make changes.

What is your train reflecting? What kind of witness are you showing to those you encounter on a day-to-day basis? You have the ability to show God's love to everyone you meet. It can be in the smallest of ways, but every time you serve another person, you are the hands and feet of Jesus in their life. Never forget that this is both a great responsibility and a great blessing.

The Abandoned Child

James was sitting at his office desk with his loyal dachshund, Flash sleeping near his feet. At fifty-two, James is a very prominent architect known worldwide for his unique, eye-catching structures. In architectural magazines, his work has been classified as "masterpieces" of art.

On the other hand, her neighbors had known Flash for having an obsession with chasing squirrels in her backyard.

James peered outside the study window at the pristine backyard with green grass and Italian cypresses lining the back fence. He sighed and focused his attention on the profit and loss sheet of his family's pharmacy business. Three years ago, after the car wreck that took his parents' lives, he inherited the business. His parents, Bill and Dotti, were both pharmacists who opened a pharmacy together thirty-eight years ago. Their pharmacy was doing very well until the competition moved in. The large chain pharmacies were focused more on volume than on customer service. An offer for the family business sat on James' desk. He was contemplating the proposal and considering a counter offer. The pharmacy was ideally located, but James never had an interest in pharmacy.

James left the report on his desk and went to get another cup of coffee. Flash ran through the kitchen and dashed through the doggy door. James stopped in front of the picture of his parent's pharmacy opening day. It brought back fond memories of the hours he spent after school there.

James made some eggs and bacon and placed some in Flash's bowl.

After the dishes were done, he grabbed Flash's leash and headed for the front door. Flash wagging her tail with excitement by her master's side.

James decided to take a different route. It had been a year since he passed through this neighborhood. New homes have been erected amongst the old ones. Flash's snout to the ground was leading the way.

At the end of the street on the left-hand side, stood his old church. He remembered his parents taking him every Sunday over the years.

As James looked over the almost empty parking lot, thoughts of his parents came to mind. After church service, his parents would wait patiently while playing with his friends in the church playground. James noticed the playground was no longer there. It was now a small-fenced cemetery with its worn, chain-linked fence. James sat on the small cement bench while Flash licked drops from a nearby leaking faucet. James sat gazing over the graveyard; Flash sat next to his master's feet, panting. James was unaware of the pastor entering the cemetery until Flash alerted him. He was deep in thought over the London project—once complete, it will be the most extensive public library in the UK.

"James," Pastor Jim said with a stretched-out hand. "How are you? I am Pastor Jim. I remember you when you were just a small boy. I have been following your success in the newspapers. Your parents were very proud of you." He bent down to scratch Flash behind the ears, "Who is this?"

"This is Flash. My rescue," James said as he shifted over on the bench to accommodate the pastor.

The two men talked. James informed Pastor Jim of the London project and the project he just completed in Chicago. The pastor sat listening intently to James describing his structural creations in detail. The pastor then updated James on his community outreach programs while giving Flash a back rub. Before the two men parted ways, the pastor encouraged James to attend church in the morning. James agreed and commented, "It has been years since my last visit."

James entered the back of the church the next morning. It was packed. Despite running a few minutes late, he had only missed the choir singing. The pastor opened his service with prayer and stated his sermon title, "The New Epidemic."

As the pastor spoke, James found himself admiring the beautiful stained glass windows. He wondered if the other two services were this packed.

"We have taken the Ten Commandments out of the courthouses. We have taken the Bible out of schools, and they sit on shelves at home. We are no longer reading our Bibles daily. Churches are closing worldwide," the pastor stated.

As the pastor continued his sermon, James thought about his London downtown project. He caught the pastor's words, "Spiritual famine...Matthew 7:14 (KJV) says, 'Because straight is the gate, and narrow is the way, which leadeth unto life, and few there be that find it.' Let us go back to serving Christ."

James went back to his project. Once again, his thoughts were interrupted by the pastor: *"Now that you have purified yourselves by obeying the truth so that you have sincere love for each other, love one another deeply, from the heart"* (1 Peter 1:22).

The man of God then said, "Let us close in prayer." He smiled as he glanced at the congregation and bowed his head.

James came back to reality, bowed his head in prayer too. After the service, he picked up the church bulletin, stood in line to exit, and shook the pastor's hand.

Tuesday morning found James looking over the blueprints on his home desk in preparation for the London project. Flash again was at his feet.

James' cellphone rang. The incoming call registered as an unknown number.

He answered the phone and heard Pastor Jim on the other end.

"James! Make sure you pack a heavy coat. London is cold this time of year. Do you need me to check on Flash while you are gone? She is welcome to stay with me."

"Thanks for the offer, but Flash is scheduled for doggy camp. She loves playing with the other dogs. Yes, warm clothes are packed and an umbrella too. How are you?"

"I am fine. I am calling to inquire if you have time for lunch before your trip?"

James accepted the invitation with pleasure.

Glancing down on the floor at the church bulletin next to him, he picked it up. He thumbed through it. The sanctuary and school rooms needed to be expanded, but noticed the lack of funding. At the top of the bulletin was a section entitled: New Mission For this Year—3:16

Interesting! What is the meaning of 3:16? He needed to ask the pastor over lunch.

Noon came quickly the next day. James was packed, and Flash was dropped off at doggy camp. All the blueprints were packed and ready for the eight-day trip to London to start the project. James had a two-and-a-half hour lunch with Pastor Jim. After ordering, the men had small talk over appetizers.

After a few bites of the main course, James commented, "I noticed the church playground is now a graveyard. How did that come about?"

"Yes. It was a unanimous decision to use that space for a small cemetery. That was so many years ago. How time flies! James—I am going to change the subject. You never mentioned a wife or children?"

"No, pastor. I have dated over the years, but nothing serious. Children? No..." as he looked down at his plate. "Talking about children, did you know I was adopted?"

"Yes. Your parents mentioned that, but they loved you as their own. They were so proud of you and very protective."

"Too protective," James said as they both laughed. "By the way, the church bulletin mentioned a 3:16 project. What does that actually mean?"

Pastor Jim stated, "John 3:16 says 'For God so loved the world that he gave his one and only Son, that whoever believes in him shall not perish but have eternal life.'" He then explained the verse in detail while handing James a Bible across the table. "This should be your blueprint for life."

While eating dessert, the pastor asked James, "I have a personal question as your pastor. How is your spiritual walk?"

James put his head down as he said, "I am struggling. I have a void in my life despite my success."

"James, I have been following your career in the newspapers for years. Your parents were so proud of you," as he smiled at James. "If you read the church bulletin, we are struggling with funds to expand the sanctuary and classrooms. Would you be willing to donate your time and expertise to complete this project? It is for God's kingdom. Just think about it."

"And the financial backing?" James asked.

"We don't have the financial resources, James," the pastor replied as he looked into James' eyes.

"Let me think about it. Let us have lunch when I get back from London," James said, reaching for the bill.

As James walked to the car, Bible in hand, he was taken aback by the proposal. No resources, he thought. But he remembered his parents frequently said, "Trust and give to the Lord. You come into this world empty-handed and leave empty-handed." He fondly remembered his parents donating to the community above and beyond their tithe.

What was that verse his father kept mentioning? Perhaps I need to put my full trust in God, James thought.

Over the next eight days, James dove into the Bible daily, reading, praying, and listening to old sermons from Pastor Jim online. Perhaps the void in my life could be filled with this new church project. He started praying about it and reflected on the Bible verse he read that morning.

"Trust in the LORD forever, for the LORD, the LORD himself, is the Rock eternal" (Isa. 26:4).

When James returned from London, he called the pastor inviting him to lunch.

"James. I would love to go to lunch with you. How was your trip?"

With excitement in his voice, "Pastor Jim! We broke ground on the project. I have a great crew. The weather was awful though," as Flash barked in the background.

"I hear Flash. Look forward to hearing details."

The two men finalized lunch plans and said their goodbyes.

Over lunch the next day, James agreed to do the church project. The pastor was overjoyed at the news. James would have to do the expansion and improvements his way. He explained he would sell the family pharmacy to fund the project.

The pastor chimed in, "I remember stopping by the pharmacy many times over the years. I know how difficult this decision was for you."

James said," I feel my parents would approve of my decision to sell their business."

The pastor agreed.

Church services were held at another local church as James began his project. Flash was equipped with a yellow shirt and helmet, both perfectly fitted, which she wore when she was on the construction site.

Eight months later, the church project was nearing completion. James was back in London when he got the call.

Pastor Peter informed him of Pastor's Jim passing. He was ill for some time, unknown to James during their almost weekly luncheons when he was in town.

James flew back to the states for the funeral service. Pastor Peter performed the service. After the funeral, James introduced himself. The small talk led Pastor Peter to ask James to accompany him to Pastor Jim's office.

"Please, have a seat James," as he gestured to the leather chair across from Pastor Jim's desk.

Pastor Peter sat behind the desk and looked at James as he handed him the gift bag. "This is from Pastor Jim. He left specific instructions to open the gift box before opening the letter. Pastor Jim would call me and share the amazing transformation you were doing with the church."

At home, James sat on the sofa with Flash at his side. Flash put her head in the bag to see if there was anything to eat. No such luck! James reached for the small, wrapped box. As he unwrapped the gift, his thoughts were that he never had the chance to say goodbye.

The box contained a worn watch. The time was perfect as he compared the reading with his iPhone. James took a deep breath before opening the envelope.

During sermons and luncheons with James, Pastor Jim commented multiple times, looking at his watch, that life is just a vapor and would quote James 4:14:

"Why, you do not even know what will happen tomorrow. What is your life? You are a mist that appears for a little while and then vanishes."

James opened the note.

> *Dear James,*
>
> *Enclosed, you will find my watch, passed on from generation to generation in my family—from father to his son over the years. I am passing it to you. I had a longing to tell you, but I didn't want it to interfere with your decision to take on the church project. I am your biological father. Your mother and I were only teenagers when you were born. We were encouraged by our parents to give you up for*

adoption. We had no financial means to support you. This last year we spent together, especially the weekly luncheons and updates on the church project, were priceless. No words can describe how overjoyed I am to see you grow spiritually and your passion for completing the "church project." Remember always: there will be no greater love than the love Christ has for you.
Love,
Pastor Jim

P.S. I noticed you came in late to church. This watch should come in handy.

John 15:13: "Greater love has no one than this: to lay down one's life for one's friends."

Leaving the Past Behind

Seventy-one-year-old Blaire walked along the beach in this tiny fishing town in the northeastern part of the United States. She was being accompanied by her thirteen-year-old black and brown dachshund, Dixie. The sun would set in an hour.

Blaire retired three years ago as CEO of a Fortune 500 company in New York City. After the death of her husband of thirty-five years, she could no longer endure staying in the apartment they shared. The memories were just too strong.

A former coworker of Blaire recommended visiting this small coastal town after her husband's death to get away, and she immediately fell in love with it. She bought a two-bedroom cottage that was walking distance from the town's local shops, diner, the lighthouse, and popular fishing dock for the locals and tourists.

This afternoon, Blaire was walking towards the dock as she did daily with Dixie, just in time for dinner at the local diner. The local diner and coffee shop welcomed Dixie with a water bowl, treats, and a little bed.

"Hi Blaire! Hi Dixie!" Tom said as he waved at Blaire. Dixie ran to Tom to get her daily back rubs. Tom, a retired physician, also widowed, fished daily on the dock. He would sit hours on his foldable chair and cushion, waiting for something to bite. He befriended Blaire three years ago when she bought the cottage.

"Doing well, Tom. Dinner on me tomorrow. Okay?" as Blaire looked into Tom's deep blue eyes.

"Of course. Two-year celebration. Right?" Tom said, smiling with his white pearly teeth.

Dixie was looking over the edge of the dock.

Blaire called Dixie as she said goodbye to Tom. Blaire found Tom to be very charming, funny, smart, caring, and handsome.

After dinner at the diner, Blaire and Dixie walked past the now-lit lighthouse near the start of the dock. They walked the paved street home, which led to her cottage. She could still hear the loud music coming from the local bar, mostly frequented by tourists.

Once home, Dixie ran to the kitchen to her water bowl and then hopped into her bed next to Blaire. After dinner and the walk home, the evening ritual was to get ready for bed and snuggle up in bed with a good book.

The light from the lighthouse shone through Blaire's bedroom shutter. She never needed a nightlight.

The next evening, Tom and Blaire enjoyed a lovely dinner at the diner.

"Tom. Thank you for caring," Blaire lifting her water glass and hit Tom's.

"My pleasure," Tom said as he smiled at Blaire.

After dinner, Tom walked Blaire and Dixie home along the paved road and kissed Blaire on her cheek. He wished her a good evening and bent over and petted Dixie behind the ear.

As Blaire settled into bed that evening, she thought about Tom and what he did two years ago for her.

You see, Tom walked to the dock every morning to go fishing. He noticed Blaire's recycling bin, which stood just inside her white picket fence full of empty wine bottles.

Tom thought over and over about the quote from Edmund Burke—*"The only thing necessary for the triumph of evil is for good men to do nothing."*

This happens often, and it's a shame. We see evil all around us, and yet we choose to do nothing. It may be out of fear, busyness, or lack of conviction, but it happens nonetheless. No matter how bold we need to be, we must do whatever it takes to help those in need. That is the foundation of what it means to be a follower of

Christ. We must be willing to stand up and fight evil and oppression in the world.

Over time, Tom got the courage to talk to Blaire about her drinking. He encouraged her to seek treatment for alcoholism, which she developed after the death of her husband. They discussed that several prescription medications were available that could be used to reduce cravings. So, Blaire admitted herself to an alcohol rehabilitation program, started medication, and has been sober for two years because of Tom's intervention.

Instead of running from her problem, Blaire fought her demons and won with Tom's help.

A quote came to Blaire's mind:

"Alcohol is the perfect solvent: It dissolves marriages, families, and careers."—Sandeep Kashiwal

Addiction is real no doubt, but many have conquered it through the grace of God. Our addictions do not have the final say over us, but God does. Even when we have control over our drinking and enjoy an occasional drink, we must never do anything that would cause someone else to stumble on their path.

In closing, the only drink that should be consumed in abundance is that of "living water."

"Jesus answered her, 'If you knew the gift of God and who it is that asks you for a drink, you would have asked him, and he would have given you living water'" (John 4:10).

You need Jesus to continue on. In the darkest times of your life, you need not turn to alcohol or anything else that helps you escape reality. You must instead drink deeply of the living water. Instead of sending you spiraling deeper and deeper into depression and ruin, living water will bring you healing. It will flow through your body, filling your soul and leading you to a place of restoration.

Think of the places you normally run to. Is it not usually back to the thing that had you addicted in the first place? Many will turn to alcohol to drown out the problems that alcoholism causes them in the first place. Others will return to an unhealthy relationship to try and mask the pain caused by that relationship in the past. The list is endless. But God has set us free in every way. Freedom from sin means never having to return to the things that have hurt us to find fleeting comfort. Instead, we can turn to God, who will offer us true peace and comfort.

Feeling Abandoned

I made an appointment with the funeral home for a pre-planning meeting for myself. Now, when the time comes, my sister only needs to call the funeral home, and they will take care of the rest. We are mortal beings in preparation for eternity. Rev. Billy Graham said it well: *"My home is in Heaven. I am just traveling through this world."* We mustn't make the mistake of living as if what we have in this world is everything. What we have here is just the beginning. God has promised us eternity with Jesus.

As I was leaving the funeral home, I saw the vast cemetery behind me. The mausoleum was in the distance. My thoughts went to Catherine. I recently met her when I was visiting a longtime friend. We spoke for an hour or so. Catherine is in her mid-fifties; she's single, a marathon runner, enjoys the outdoors, and loves to scuba dive. She is fit and very much aware of her appearance. While we were chatting, I could see the compassion she had for animals when she was playing with my dachshund. But her love for animals goes beyond that. It includes the welfare of all animals.

Our conversation led to work. Catherine has worked in several roles through the years with her master's degree in Outpatient Surgery, Hospice Care, and Quality Control. She is also a caring person who always helps others. When Catherine commented on her large family of six sisters, I couldn't imagine the family dynamics.

My thoughts went to Catherine because she recently lost her mother to the COVID virus. She considers herself an orphan after the loss of both parents now. Anger, denial, and overwhelming sadness flooded her inner being as waves pound the shore during a storm.

We have to anchor our hope on 2 Corinthians 5:8: *"to be absent from the body, and to be present with the Lord."* When the storms of life rage and we are being tossed about, we can't rely on our own power. We can only hold ourselves upright for so long. But God is stronger than anything we will ever face. When we live out our lives in a relationship with Him, there's nothing that can stand in our way. He fills us with immeasurable hope.

Hebrews 6:19 reads, *"We have this hope as an anchor for the soul, firm and secure."* The word anchor is important here. An anchor ensures that a boat does not drift away on chaotic waters. It keeps the boat firmly in place. The hope that God provides is an anchor for our soul. When the waters of life surround us and crash against us, the hope that God provides makes it so that we will not be moved. We will be strong and rooted in the Lord.

The first anchor in a crisis is the presence of God. Storms can never hide us from God. We may not see Him, but He sees us. We may think God is a million miles away, but He is with us and is watching us."—Rick Warren

God never leaves us abandoned. Even when it seems as if we are all alone, we can rest assured that He is by our side. All we must do is seek Him, and He will respond to our prayers. In Jeremiah 29:12–13, God says, *"In those days when you pray, I will listen. If you look for me wholeheartedly, you will find me"* (NLT). When you walk with the Lord, you are never alone.

"Although we may trust God's promises for life after death, and the certainty of a heavenly home, we must face the reality of death."—Rev. Billy Graham

Just because God has promised us eternity doesn't mean that He takes all of our trials away in this life. God's promises are true, and knowing that helps give us the strength to persevere.

Months following the death of Catherine's mom, I wanted to take Catherine away from the stress of work. I invited her along on my vacation with two other college friends of mine. The cottage I rented had an extra bedroom and bath we weren't going to use. I prayed that it would be a chance for her to find the rest and rejuvenation I knew she so desperately needed.

Fast forward to the present on the Atlantic Ocean:

I sat on a beach towel on a twenty-eight-foot boat, waiting on Catherine and her scuba partner to come up from the ocean. This scuba excursion started before dawn and was supposed to end by lunchtime. It was well past that now. My stomach started to growl, and my thoughts were to raid the bag full of snacks that I brought with me.

I never had an interest in scuba diving, but I told Catherine I would accompany her on this one diving trip. A scuba-diving friend of mine says it is an equipment-intensive sport in order to maintain your life underwater. Of course I see it as an exciting endeavor. There are various diving sites around the world, where you journey into the unknown below. The infinite marine beauty, unexplored caves, coral reefs, the ships and planes that have fallen into the sea are all at one's disposal. It is a gorgeous world one should visit, or so I've been told.

As the boat rocked and seagulls squawked overhead, Catherine nor her scuba partner were anywhere in sight. I heard the faint cling, clang, cling from the large bell at the base of the lighthouse on the shore. I decided to find refuge under the boat canopy from the hot, beating sun. The ice-cold water in the cooler was very refreshing. Fortunately, this twenty-eight-foot boat had a bathroom on board.

While I was scanning the horizon, I noticed there were no boats to be seen. My thoughts went back to Catherine and all the scuba gear (oxygen tank, scuba suit, flippers, underwater lights) she brought on this trip. When scuba diving, one must be continuously aware of one's bearings and the oxygen supply remaining in one's tank during the dive. How peaceful it must be under the water!

"Hey! You okay?" shouted Catherine from the surface.

I glanced in her direction. Her face mask was pulled up on top of her head.

"Doing fine. Thanks," I said while standing and looking over the edge of the boat at her.

"I want to explore a little more. I got some great pictures to show you of some wreckage. My air tank has forty minutes left," Catherine stated as she dove under the water again.

The sunbeams were now shining through the clouds as the wind was picking up. The boat was rocking more. I glanced at my watch. As we dive into the depths of life, we need to take the time to appreciate the infinite beauty that surrounds us, but especially our family and friends. And as we walk out of the ocean of life with the heavy scuba gear (joke) on our backs from our underwater excursion (activities), the heavy burdens we carry in life need to be placed at the foot of the cross. The one thing we need to pick up is hope.

"God never promises to remove us from our struggles. He does promise, however, to change the way we look at them."—Max Lucado

Faith gives us perspective. Once we enter a relationship with Christ, we never see the world the same way again. He reshapes our hearts, minds, and attitude so that it aligns with His will. This newfound outlook on life helps us to make it through the trials because we know we are not walking through them alone. God often has something to teach us in our most trying moments, but we'll only see it if our hearts are aligned with His.

Abandoned Character

Judy and Claire had been working together at the local police department for five years. Judy has six additional years of rank ahead of Claire. Judy is Claire's boss and a forty-three-year-old private detective.

"Claire, look at this file, please," said Judy.

As Claire opened the folder, there was one sheet of paper on top of several photographs.

On the paper was written:

Crime scene: *At the Double O Pharmaceutical Company on the second floor of the building*
Time of death: *Approximately 9:00 p.m. on April 16th*
Any witnesses: *None*
No surveillance cameras either
No fingerprints found
Victim: *Dr. Andrew (researcher)*

CEO of the Double O Pharmaceutical Company: *Mr. Bruce*

CFO: *Mrs. Ann*

Double O Pharmaceutical Company employs 12 people (1 researcher, 8 technicians, 1 secretary, 1 CEO, and 1 CFO)

Research: *Cancer treatments*

Claire then glanced at the photographs to discover Dr. Andrew was shot in the head, close range. All other photos reflected the countertops of his lab and windows.

Nothing appears out of order, Claire thought.

Claire closed the folder and looked at Judy.

"Were there no cameras whatsoever inside or outside the building, or perhaps across the street?" Claire asked as she handed the folder back to Judy.

"Surveillance was turned off in this two-story building. We are retrieving the footage from the cameras across the street," Judy stated as she was leaning on Claire's desk.

She added, "We have an appointment with the CFO and CEO this afternoon. I need you to research the background on them both before the meeting. Also, check all the technicians and exactly what they were researching. Thanks." Judy headed for her desk. She turned around and said, "I have already requested the financial statements for the company."

"How about the business contracts and any enemies Dr. Andrew may have had? Has that been researched?" Claire asked Judy.

"I'm on it," she said as she took a seat at her desk.

Judy briefed Claire on her findings. Claire returned the favor during their drive over to the Double O Pharmaceutical Company.

They conducted the interview with the CFO and CEO. They also studied the business contracts and financial reports. Altogether, it took them four-and-a-half hours.

Claire sighed.

Claire was getting tired from reading the movie script, so she placed it on her nightstand. She was only a quarter of the way through the manuscript as she reflected on the detective movie role. It was probably greed that led to the murder.

That is precisely what happened to Judas in the Bible. Greed got the best of him.

But one of his disciples, Judas Iscariot, who was later to betray him, objected, "Why wasn't this perfume sold and the money given to the poor? It was worth a year's wages." He did not say this because he cared about the poor but because he was a thief;

*as keeper of the money bag, he used to help himself
to what was put into it.*

John 12:4–6

He manipulated situations for his benefit. He used the ministry he was a part of to swindle money from the poor. He walked with Jesus Himself. He may have had good intentions at one point, but still, he let greed consume him. This is true of many villains in books, TV shows, and movies. Greed always seems to get the better of us. Claire figured that just like Judas, the murder in the script was likewise provoked by greed. It always was.

Suddenly, her cellphone began to ring. She took it from her nightstand and looked at the caller ID. It was her film agent at this late hour.

Before she could say hello, Mark asked with enthusiasm in his voice, "Well, what did you think of the movie script?"

"I had a late start. So far, so good. I have read the first fifty pages. What is the conclusion?" Claire asked.

"You will find out that the CFO is the daughter of the CEO. She (the CFO) was plotting to kill her father too. Basically greed. She then escapes from prison," Mark said.

"Escapes from prison? Let me guess? She comes after Judy and me because she has nothing to lose with a life sentence already," Claire said, laughing.

"Exactly. I need an answer by noon tomorrow if you want to play the role of the detective. The film director wants to start filming in three weeks," Mark said.

"Let me sleep on it. I will call you in the morning. Night!" She said as she hung up her cellphone and placed it back on her nightstand. She gently pushed her rescue Rottweiler mix named Maggie to the other side of the bed.

Escapes from prison to get revenge on those that put her there. Hmmm...revenge ran through her mind as she reviewed the movie script in her head again.

"Do not take revenge, my dear friends, but leave room for God's wrath, for it is written: 'It is mine to avenge; I will repay,' says the Lord" (Rom. 12:19).

As she turned off the lights and gently pushed Maggie further to the other side, the "little one," as she called her, got quite grumpy for being awakened.

She again thought about the detectives in the movie script. They searched for lost children for an extended period and sowed their lives into solving murder cases, etc. Detectives must keep their eyes open so they won't overlook any clues. As Christians, we must keep an eye on what really matters in life. Today, society's obsession with money and revenge often leads to a dark path.

"For the love of money is the root of all kinds of evil. Some people, eager for money, have wandered from the faith and pierced themselves with many griefs" (1 Tim. 6:10).

In Matthew 6:21, Jesus says, *"For where your treasure is, there your heart will be also."* Our hearts are swayed by the things we hold most dear. When money or possessions occupy our hearts and minds, our character can be compromised. We may do things we would never otherwise do in order to protect those things. Sadly, we abandon our character out of greed.

As Claire adjusted her pillow, she stretched her legs and accidentally hit Maggie. She growled.

Claire started laughing.

While making coffee the next morning, she left the movie script on the kitchen table. Many thoughts came to mind as she poured her first cup of coffee. The scene in the boardroom, when the detectives were interviewing the father and daughter, as CEO and CFO respectively, ran through her mind. The researcher killed over money.

Generally, members of any board should be people with excellent reputation and knowledge.

It reminded her of the saying by Thomas Paine: *"Reputation is what men and women think about us; character is what God and angels know of us.."*

Having a good reputation doesn't always mean you have good character. We must always focus on our character first. It will determine our actions and way of life. Our character is built by faith as we walk through life alongside God.

"When wealth is lost, nothing is lost; when health is lost, something is lost; when character is lost, all is lost." —Rev. Billy Graham

Our character defines who we are. When we live as children of God, it is reflected in our character. How we treat others, how we steward our resources, and how we generally live our lives is all dictated by our character. We must focus on building it around God's teachings, living out our faith, and showing Christ's love to others.

"Your character is the harvest of your habits." —Adrian Rogers

As Claire pondered the movie script, she imagined the scene when she accompanied the father (the CEO) to the "prison visitation." She leaned against the wall at a distance as the father sits across from his daughter with a glass partition dividing them. As she observes the conversation, the daughter slams both fists against the counter with anger in her face as her father wipes his tears with a handkerchief. He sits in silence as tears run down his face.

Just observe how this father in this movie script was so moved to tears by his daughter's sin. Just think what our heavenly Father feels when we fail to repent of our sins.

Abandoned Mercy

Bruce is a thirty-two-year-old who occupies the bottom bunk in his prison cell. He spends twenty-one hours out of the day in his cell. He is able to spend some time working out, playing basketball, and cleaning the canteen after meals. Bruce is three years into his eighteen-year prison sentence for murder. His cellmate, Jake, is twenty-one years old. Jake is in prison for stealing multiple cars from local dealerships. He has eight years remaining in his ten-year sentence. Jake and Bruce haven't spoken much since becoming cellmates one year ago. It is supposedly due to Jake's conversion. Bruce considers Jake a religious freak, thanks to the prison ministry.

Jake has been encouraging Bruce to attend the twice-weekly Bible study to no avail. Bruce kept telling his cellmate, "I don't understand you, Jesus freak."

Bruce has had underlying anger issues over the years, and it is quite apparent when he talks about his past. Jake slowly started sharing Bible verses about anger with Bruce before bedtime.

He would often quote Psalms 37:8:

"Refrain from anger and turn from wrath; do not fret—it leads only to evil."

And Proverbs 29:22:

"An angry person stirs up conflict, and a hot-tempered person commits many sins."

Three months went by, and more scripture about anger was discussed amongst the two of them. Jake continued to pray for Bruce's conversion. Then, one day, Bruce agreed to go to the Bible study.

He was greeted with a warm welcome by Billy, a fifty-seven-year-old deacon from the local church, who had been leading a Bible study at the prison for eleven years.

All the inmates sat at a long plastic lunch table in plastic chairs.

Billy started the Bible study with prayer and then opened with the following Bible verse: *"In your anger, do not sin: Do not let the sun go down while you are still angry, and do not give the devil a foothold"* (Eph. 4:26–27).

Billy was talking about his past anger issues and how his anger was finally released by forgiveness. Then, he started with the story that was the beginning of it all.

Out of the blue, Bruce stood up and slammed his chair against the table. He shouted, "Billy! What do you know about forgiveness? I don't want your God."

Deacon Billy thought that Bruce just abandoned mercy.

The prison guard suddenly grabbed Bruce by his shackles and escorted him out of the room to his cell.

Jake didn't know what to expect when he would return to his cell later. Fortunately, Bruce was snoring when he got there.

Weeks went by, and Bruce never mentioned the Bible study. Tuesday rolled around again, and Jake didn't go to Bible study.

"What's up? No Bible study today, Jake? That is a first for you," Bruce said sarcastically.

"Deacon Billy died. Heart attack," Jake said sorrowfully.

"Oh," Bruce replied.

"Do you remember when you attended the one Bible study that you had your outburst?" Jake said with a touch of concern.

"Yeah, what about it? I remember. Billy was talking about anger and how he forgave. And?" Bruce said with anger in his voice.

"Well, you didn't hear the end of his story," Jake said with curiosity wondering if Bruce would be at all interested.

"I am listening," Bruce said with a touch of frustration in his voice.

Jake cleared his throat, "Years ago, Deacon Billy went over to his sister's house for Easter lunch after the service."

Jake glanced at Bruce to see if he was paying attention. Their eyes locked.

Jake continued, "Well, he went through the garage door, which was always left open when Jill, his sister, was home. He opened the screen door and discovered the wooden door that led to the kitchen was unlocked. Deacon Billy called his sister's name several times, but she didn't respond. He later found her in the master bedroom, murdered. Four days after the murder, the police had a suspect in custody. They apprehended one Mr. Bruce, age twenty-nine. You!"

"All this time, Bruce, I never knew you were the one who killed Deacon Billy's sister. But, you know what? He genuinely forgave you."

Bruce looked at Jake without any remorse or comment. He proceeded to sit on his bunk, grabbed a magazine, and started flipping through it.

"Anger is an acid that can do more harm to the vessel in which it is stored than to anything on which it is poured."— Mark Twain

We must be careful to control our anger. It is natural to find ourselves in situations where we may become angry, but we must find healthy ways to reel it in. When we let anger stew and fester, it grows and grows until it begins to control us. Anger has a way of escalating, and there becomes a point when it grows completely out of our control.

At that point, our anger starts determining our actions. We begin to do things that we'd never do otherwise. We begin to leave a trail of broken relationships in our path, and we never grow in life. When things start to get that bad, the anger hardens our hearts. The further we slip down that slippery slope, the harder it is to reach us. There sadly becomes a point where we become like Bruce.

James 1:19 says, *"My dear brothers and sisters, take note of this: Everyone should be quick to listen, slow to speak, and slow to become angry."* Even when we are feeling angry, we should always take the time to listen and think carefully before we speak. Like Bruce, we may be missing something powerful when we speak out in anger. When that happens, we may never get the chance to hear it again. In Bruce's case, it was information that may have well changed his life. Mercy has a way of doing that.

Consider what your future will look like given two scenarios.

You Let Your Anger Consume You

When you go this route, you'll likely lose many precious things along the way. Your relationships, career, and even your life could be in jeopardy. The more that anger fills your heart, the less you'll be able to experience joy in your life. Things that you used to love will not be fulfilling and enjoyable anymore. You'll continually hurt yourself and those closest to you. That's no way to live! That is not the kind of life that God desires for His children to live.

You Put Your Anger in God's Hand and Accept His Joy and Peace

When you do this, you'll be able to release your anger once and for all. It will never control you again. When you place it in God's hands, He will take it away for good. Your faith will thrive. You'll find the joy and enthusiasm in life necessary to live out God's calling for your life. Never again will you be weighed down by the burdens that shackled you before. Which will you choose? The choice is yours to make today.

Life and Death

There are six things the LORD hates, seven that are detestable to him: haughty eyes, a lying tongue, hands that shed innocent blood, a heart that devises wicked schemes, feet that are quick to rush into evil, a false witness who pours out lies and a person who stirs up conflict in the community.

Proverbs 6:16–19

The school auditorium was filling up on a winter evening. Sleet was in the forecast. The local television and radio stations advertised this speaker all week. It appears this seventy-six-year-old was touring the United States and Canada to any audience open to listening to his story, "Life and Death."

Meg sat in the second row in the middle of the auditorium with her mother, Anita by her side. The speaker appeared on stage on the far left. He put his microphone on his lapel and looked at the screen as it rolled down with a remote in his right hand.

The speaker cleared his throat and said, *"Good evening. I am so happy you could join me on this cold, gloomy evening. I am Reed T from southern Alabama. People call me RT."*

The speaker was over six feet tall, bald, with a well-groomed goatee, stylish glasses with blue khakis, a white button-down shirt, with a matching blue sports jacket.

"Many may know my story and cause, but for those that don't, let me begin," he said as he glanced at the screen. A young RT in blue jeans and a University of Alabama jersey appeared on the screen.

"I served as a medic for thirty-two years. I have seen death firsthand. In some instances, I could do nothing but comfort some."

The audience was utterly silent.

"One day, tragedy struck at home. My heart was torn out when my wife died of a brain aneurysm."

At this point, a picture of his wife was shown on the screen.

"Mary, my wife of nine years. This picture was taken a few months before her death."

"This is Sarah, my daughter," he said as he glanced at the screen. RT smiled as he glanced at the picture of a brunette with shoulder-length hair flashing a contagious smile. *"She is forty-four years old now and works as a physician assistant in an OB/GYN office."*

"My purpose in life now is because of Sarah, who interned at a doctor's office and shared her stories with me over her three-month internship. Her unbelievable stories filled my mind for days and were proven true when we drove to the doctor's office one evening. Behind the building, Sarah showed me exactly what was going on. She opened one bag which had not been picked up yet by the medical waste services. Aborted fetuses, some still intact. Hands, feet, face...all purple now and in different sizes. Other fetuses were dismembered."

RT took a sip of water and glanced around the audience.

"My stomach turned that night on the way home, and I had weeks of sleepless nights. Psalm 100:3 says, 'Know that the LORD is God. It is he who made us, and we are his; we are his people, the sheep of his pasture.' God never does anything accidentally, and He never makes mistakes," according to Rick Warren.

RT took a sip of water and continued:

"For I know the plans I have for you," declares the LORD, *"plans to prosper you and not to harm you, plans to give you hope and a future"* according to Jeremiah 29:11.

He sighed.

"Dr. Tony Evans of Dallas, Texas, who serves as senior pastor of Oak Cliff Bible Fellowship, once said, 'When you take someone's life, you also take away their right to liberty and their pursuit of happiness. If you take someone's life, you

also take their dreams, their future, their family, and their career.'"

RT glanced around the auditorium and adjusted his stance.

"It is interesting, if you hit and kill a pregnant woman, one can be charged with the wrongful death of the mother and fetus in most states. Yes—an unborn child killed in an automobile accident—one can be charged with wrongful death. Think about that for a minute."

"Okay. Back to my story," RT said, "I took it upon myself to go behind the abortion clinic dumpster to take the aborted babies and give them an appropriate burial."

"Long story. I approached a local cemetery about my plans. But my goal is to do this nationwide."

RT stated, "Once alive and growing and now dead. They deserve respect. They are not trash. If you are considering an abortion, please consider what George H. W. Bush once said. Let us put politics aside and just focus on what he once said, 'Adoption was such a positive alternative to abortion, a way to save one life and brighten two: those of the adoptive parents.'"

"Did you know that Dave Thomas, the founder of Wendy's hamburgers chain, was adopted? So was Steve Jobs, one of the cofounders of Apple. There are many famous people who have been adopted. Many may not know who their biological parents are, but you can know your Heavenly Father. Jeremiah 1:5 reads, "For before I formed you in the womb I knew you, *before you were born I set you apart; I appointed you as a prophet to the nations."*

"Let's not forget Jesus... *'Behold, the virgin shall be with child and shall bear a Son, and they shall call His name Immanuel'"* (Luke 1:27).

Joseph, the future husband of Mary, adopted Jesus as his own son. He was not Jesus' biological father. No one in his own time would have faulted him for walking away when Mary was found to be pregnant. Many others would have. But Joseph knew that there was value in Mary and Jesus alike. He chose to take Jesus as his own son instead of casting him aside.

Ephesians 1:5 says, *"He predestined us for adoption to himself as sons through Jesus Christ, according to the purpose of his will." In the same way, God accepts us no matter what our situation. God takes us in as sons and daughters. He is unlike any other and will care for us and love us. He values every life and will never forsake or abandon you.*

"*I would like to close with this,"* RT said as he looked at the screen again at a picture of a young woman. *"This young lady changed my life. She rocks my world: my thirty-year-old granddaughter, Samantha. My daughter contemplated an abortion at the age of fourteen, but I discouraged her from going through with it. Samantha is now a physician with Physicians without Borders. She goes around the world helping those in need."*

"Thanks for your time tonight. I will leave the website of my foundation on the screen if anyone is interested in donating to my cause."

As RT was removing the microphone from his lapel, Meg and Anita sat in silence. Many people were standing up and working their way to RT, who was now making his way to the auditorium floor.

Psalm 24:1 reads, *"The earth is the LORD's, and everything in it, the world, and all who live in it."* We never have the right to throw a life away. All life belongs to God. No matter what stage of life they are in, every person is inherently valuable because they were created in God's image. God loves each and every one of us unconditionally, and He calls us to do the same.

Abandoned News

It's gloomy outside. The black clouds have been dumping rain for the last several hours. Before the downpour, the wind was blowing mist off the grass. The trees are slowly revealing green leaves as panic and anxiety fill the air due to the new COVID-19 pandemic. The stock market is tanking, churches are closing, and the news is broadcasting there are not enough ventilators and masks to go around.

What would happen if God's view of the daily news hit the front page of the newspaper? What if one could scroll through the miracles and interventions God performs on a daily basis?

God wants to inspire us and fill us with hope, but we have drifted away from Him. He is at work all around us, but we refuse to see it. Our lives would be so different if we could see God's presence all around us. He does miraculous things all over the world every single day. He wants to do the unimaginable in your life as well.

Let us first look at a miracle in the Bible.

In Luke 17:11–19, Jesus heals the lepers:

> Now on his way to Jerusalem, Jesus traveled along the border between Samaria and Galilee. As he was going into a village, ten men who had leprosy met him. They stood at a distance and called out in a loud voice, "Jesus, Master, have pity on us!" When he saw them, he said, "Go, show yourselves to the priests." And as they went, they were cleansed. One of them, when he saw he was healed, came back, praising God in a loud voice. He threw himself at Jesus' feet and thanked him—and he was a Samaritan. Jesus asked, "Were not all ten cleansed? Where are the other nine? Has no one returned to give praise to God except this foreigner?" Then he said to him, "Rise and go; your faith has made you well."

There are many other miracles in the Bible. Let us look at a present-day miracle (true story).

I met Nurse Lisa during my hospitalization post-spinal surgery. She was my nurse during the day shift.

Lisa's story:

Her husband sustained a fall, which led to internal hemorrhaging in his head. During his hospitalization, his liver, kidneys, and other vital organs started shutting down. Doctors of multiple specialties wanted to have a conference with Nurse Lisa to address her husband's status. Nurse Lisa was told her husband was on life support, and she should start thinking about what she wanted to do.

Nurse Lisa knew exactly what they were saying, but she stood up from her seat in the conference room and addressed all of her husband's physicians: "I respect all of you. I thank you all for your help, but I respect my God much more."

This was either Friday or Saturday. She told the physicians she would be back on Sunday at 6:00 p.m.

Nurse Lisa proceeded to go to three or four local churches, requesting people to show up at her house on Sunday morning by 11:00 a.m. for prayer. *"We will pray until 5:00 p.m. for my husband. Food will be provided,"* she said.

At 11:00 a.m. on Sunday: Over 200 people showed up at her home—people she didn't even know.

At 6:00 p.m. on Sunday: Nurse Lisa showed up at the hospital; her husband's hospital door was closed. Her husband lost sixty pounds during this hospitalization. He was surrounded by six to seven physicians when her husband awakened and started pulling out all his tubing. He said he wanted something to eat. The physicians were baffled. God showed up.

Doubting? Even John the Baptist doubted in Luke 7:20: *When the men came to Jesus, they said, "John the Baptist sent us to you to ask, 'Are you the one who is to come, or should we expect someone else?'"*

As Christians, we need to take hold of Matthew 21:22, just like Nurse Lisa did. There is no miracle too big for God. We should never hold back in asking God for good things. Nurse Lisa intervened for her husband. God heard her prayer and responded in a big way. Lisa was bold in prayer, and God was bold in His response. We must never put a limit on what we believe God is able to do. He is the almighty God who can do anything. All we must do is believe in Him.

"If you believe, you will receive whatever you ask for in prayer" (Matt. 21:22).

Prayer is powerful. It is irreplaceable in the Christian life. Communication is the foundation of every relationship, and prayer is how we communicate with God. God is our Father, and we are His children. He wants to give nothing but good things to His children. Never doubt that He will go to unbelievable lengths to answer your prayers if only you'd seek Him.

We need to also give thanks during difficult times as it is written in 1 Thessalonians 5:18: *"In everything give thanks: for this is the will of God in Christ Jesus concerning you."* We believe that God works everything together for the good of those who believe. He has the power to bring good even out of the worst of situations. No matter what we are going through, there is always something to be thankful for. God is good, all the time.

There are three other friends of mine, not including myself, who have experienced the miraculous. Just because the news is flooded with negativity and we don't often hear of miracles happening around us doesn't mean that God isn't working in the world. We as a society are just not tuned into the right channel. All of the wonderful news of God working in people's lives worldwide is drowned out by our own fear and insecurity. God wants to fill us with hope and peace, but we have blinded ourselves to His presence in the world.

As reporters keep pouring out bad news, our Lord continues to paint the night sky with stars, gives the earth warmth, and makes the sun a source of light for us. He saturates the soil with water from rain to grow our crops. The COVID-19 virus is contagious. Let our love and kindness be infectious through these turbulent times and otherwise. Never forget the continuous presence of God.

Abandoned Gifts

"Each of you should use whatever gift you have received to serve others as faithful stewards of God's grace in its various forms" (1 Peter 4:10).

Everyone has a gift or talent. God has a plan for each one of our lives and a purpose that He has prepared for us to fulfill. He gives us unique gifts in order to see that purpose through to fruition. He wants to reveal our gifts to us, then lead us in developing that gift. Once we do, He wants to guide us to where we can live out our talent in service to others.

Sadly, some individuals decide never to pursue their gifts. They cast aside their God-given gifts or never even bother seeking them out at all. They go through life, never walking the path that they were always meant to walk. It can be because they doubt themselves, don't have a relationship with God or are unmotivated. Whatever the reason, it is a tragedy to never live out the purpose for which they were created.

It's a tragedy because even one person can make a huge impact. You never know how God's calling on your life can change the world. As we study the Bible, God's Word, we see countless stories of the unbelievable things that God has done through ordinary people like you and me.

Take the disciples, for example. They were regular people doing ordinary things. But then God showed up in their lives, and they were never the same. Jesus walked alongside them, teaching them and equipping them for ministry. The entire time, He was helping them to cultivate their gifts. When they were ready, Jesus gave them their mission and set them out into the world.

The rest is history. These normal, everyday people changed the world. They spread the gospel throughout the world, and the church they started lives on to this day.

A designer designs clothes or glasses or some other item that can change a fashion trend.

A teacher teaches students, which in turn impacts the future of that child or children.

A surgeon performs surgery to change an individual's life, who can now hopefully live a normal life or extend their life.

I have a story of someone who used their gift to impact my life.

Doreen, a longtime friend, took my then six-year-old dachshund in while I was undergoing cancer treatments and surgeries. A call from her prompted me to book a flight. My dachshund, Flash, was paralyzed after a disc in her neck slipped under another disc. She would have to undergo a difficult surgical procedure. No guarantees were made that Flash would survive the anesthesia because she had difficulty with the anesthesia during her CT scan done by Dr. Julia, who would be the veterinarian to perform the surgery. Dr. Julia, a veterinarian specializing in neurology, told Doreen that Flash would definitely be a "case" to share with other veterinarians and clients.

As I scanned Dr. Julie's reviews online, there was no question she was the perfect neurosurgical vet for Flash.

Online reviews were outstanding: caring, knowledgeable, reassuring, and wise—endless reviews of her talent.

The word "wise" reminded me of Solomon in the Bible, and this verse from the book of James: *"But the wisdom that comes from heaven is first of all pure; then peace-loving, considerate, submissive, full of mercy and good fruit, impartial and sincere"* (James 3:17).

God desires that wisdom guide us through our lives. When coupling wisdom with our gifts, incredible things can happen. Dr. Julie sounded like a woman who used her talents in wise and compassionate ways. That spoke to me. I wanted someone like that to take care of my beloved pet.

Fast forward...

Flash's surgery went well, but the recovery was still upon us. I was allowed to visit Flash a day and a half after her surgery.

During my first visit after Flash's surgery, Dr. Julie placed Flash on my lap while I sat on the sofa in the front waiting area. My back was turned to the front window as Dr. Julie sat across from me on another sofa. Dr. Julie answered all my questions. She proceeded to place a sheepskin blanket on the floor to show me some physical therapy exercises I could do with Flash in order to speed her recovery.

Dr. Julie got Flash's squeaky toy from her bed, which was behind Dr. Julie's desk. If anyone knows Flash, she has an obsession with tennis balls and squeaky toys. As Dr. Julie sat on the sheepskin blanket, she noticed Flash's squeaky toy had a hole in it. The hole was made by another dachshund who had just undergone a similar procedure as Flash. This other dachshund was now up and walking around and must have stolen it from Flash's bed. Dr. Julie got up from the floor and proceeded to get her surgical sutures to sew the hole in the squeaky toy. She proceeded to sew up the hole while I held the toy.

Humility for sure.

"Be completely humble and gentle; be patient, bearing with one another in love" (Eph. 4:2).

In using our gifts, we must not only express wisdom but humility as well. Our talents are not to help us boast or flaunt how good we are at something. God placed these gifts within us to use to help others. It is not about us, but about those in need that we can impact. When we combine our talents, wisdom, and humility, we can alter people's lives for the cause of the gospel. When you boast about your gifts or think of yourself too highly because of what you can do, you lessen the influence you have to be a witness to the gospel. No matter what your talent is, remember who gave you that gift. It was the Lord. Commit to utilizing your gift for the glory of God and not yourself.

Matthew 20:28 says, *"the Son of Man did not come to be served, but to serve."* If Jesus Himself, the only one deserving of our worship, came to serve and not be served, what reason do we have to not be humble? Jesus lived His life for the sake of others and never sought recognition for it. We should strive to emulate Him in everything that we do. He gave of Himself in every way, even to death, in order to save humanity.

Day by day, Flash made progress under Dr. Julie and her assistant's care and then under the care of my friend, Doreen. I am forever grateful for Doreen's kindness during this time of my life.

As Dr. Julie has a talent, which she is using to better the lives of pets, each of us is given a gift or talent.

As Rick Warren, pastor of Saddleback Church and author of *The Purpose Driven Life* (Make the Most of Your Talents: June 29, 2017) once said:

> *If you think your talents are simply for you to make a lot of money, retire and die, you've missed the point of life. God gave you talents to benefit others, not yourself. And God gave other people talents to benefit you.*

Unlike what the world around us tells us, we cannot do everything alone. We were created for relationships, and we were made to enrich each other's lives. One powerful way that we do this is through the natural abilities God has given us. When we share in our gifts for the furtherance of God's kingdom and the benefit of those in need, we grow as people and as the church.

Commit to bettering the lives of others and walk as Jesus walked.

The Abandoned Room in the Art Museum

One summer day, to beat the Texas heat, I decided to explore the local art museum. It has been years since I took the time to walk through the halls of this gallery. Art inspires me.

We know God as creator. He created the world and everything in it. What a masterpiece! Consider nature for a moment. There is such diversity in the world. There are lush rain forests, sprawling plains, high mountains, and oceans as far as the eye can see. Not only that, but think of all the animals. God has brought so many creatures into the world, big and small. His imagination and creativity is unmatched.

Feeling the coolness of the air-conditioned rooms against my sweaty shirt felt great. I was walking slowly across the creaky wood floors. The air smelt musty.

MICHELLE YOST & NICOLE YOST

Each room showcased security cameras as well as security guards holstering a gun on their hip. Some very valuable portraits were displayed behind bulletproof glass, with a climate-controlled environment and a laser security alarm. Fire alarm pull stations were on each wall, and multiple water sprinkler heads could be seen overhead.

I sat on the bench in front of a portrait, which displayed a man with darkened withered skin from I assume longtime exposure to the sun. With a straw hat on, the man portrayed a genuine smile for the painter. Many vibrant oil colors flowed across the canvas: deep oranges, brilliant blues, and yellows—this simple oil painting dated over 150 years.

My thoughts were interrupted by a large group entering the room with a tour guide out front talking loudly. Many children suddenly started running through this room of the museum, unaware of the value of each portrait.

My thoughts went to the portrait of the man in front of me. What if we explored the portrait from a totally different perspective? Oil paintings are a "shot in time." Generally, no touch-ups or alterations are done like some pictures we see in magazines these days. As binoculars and telescopes are used to help us see in the far distance, microscopes are used to see small items mostly unseen to the naked eye. In the medical world,

CT scans and MRI machines allow the medical staff to see inside the human body generally to detect if something is wrong. But let us say, through either a CT or MRI machine, we can examine the character of the person in the portrait?

A portrait of Jesus. What character would we find?

God is Faithful

God is always faithful to His people. We see this throughout the course of the Bible. Time and time again, humanity turns their back on God, fleeing towards fleeting pleasures instead. This is not dissimilar to our society today. The world in general is becoming more and more antagonistic towards Christianity and God. Despite it, God continues to love each and every person around the world. We see it in the Scriptures and we see it today: God remains faithful and by our side no matter what we do or say. 2 Timothy 2:13 says, *"If we are faithless, he remains faithful, for he cannot disown himself."*

In what ways is God faithful, you may ask? In every way! God will always love you, protect you, and strengthen you. He will help you grow in faith, character, and love. He has brought you into the world and invested so much into you because you are beloved to Him and unconditionally loved more than you could ever know. *"But the LORD is faithful, and he will strengthen you and protect you from the evil one"* (2 Thess. 3:3).

God is Flawless

You can always trust God, because His ways are perfect. He is the definition of purity and holiness. There is no fault in the Lord. He has existed from the beginning of time and is eternal. When you follow the Lord, you can rest assured without a shadow of a doubt that you are following the correct path in life. *"As for God, his way is perfect: The Lord's word is flawless; he shields all who take refuge in him"* (Ps. 18:30).

God is Full of Compassion

Even though God is all-powerful and holds all authority over the universe, He is not an impersonal God. God is passionate about His creation. That's precisely why He sent Jesus to come to earth, taking on the fullness of humanity.

Think about that statement for a moment. Jesus fully took on humanity. That means that He suffered through all of the bodily and worldly things that we do, just to relate to us, serve us, and ultimately die on our behalf. If that's not compassion, what is? God shows boundless compassion always. Psalm 116:5 says, *"The LORD is gracious and righteous; our God is full of compassion."*

As I got up from the bench to explore the remaining of this art exhibit, I noticed all the security cameras. I came to a room barricaded off with rope. I took a quick glance. No portraits or statues, but huge crates lined the middle of the room.

"What was in here?" I asked the security guard sitting just outside this room.

"Not a very popular exhibit. It just lasted two weeks. As a matter of fact, there were so many complaints the museum curator directed it to be taken down. It was an art exhibit which showcased the development of human life from conception to birth."

"Oh," I responded, as the security guard glanced at his phone.

I continued to walk through the museum, glancing at the various marble statues, landscape portraits, art depicting battle scenes, and the waters of the Mediterranean. Multiple of these portraits were behind the bulletproof glass.

My thoughts went back to the short-lived human life exhibit. What humans find valuable differs from what God considers valuable. For it is written in Genesis 1:26, *"Let us make mankind in our image, in our likeness."*

Descending the steps of the museum, it was misting outside as I walked to the parking lot.

When one looks at a picture, family photos, or portraits, one focuses on physical features: eyes, mouth, cheekbones, and then glances at the person's attire and the backdrop. If we look deeper beyond the superficial, we will uncover that we are very valuable in God's eyes. We were valued enough that the King of kings and LORD of lords (Rev. 19:16) died for each one of us. We are royalty in His family.

Are you interested in being in the Lord's family photo?

Abandoning the One True God

Jessica and I explored the small beach town three hours from the hustle and bustle of the city life we both lived in. We each took one week off from our jobs just to relax and enjoy the end of summer. It was a much-needed break, and wonderful to spend time together.

Jessica is a fitness guru and scuba diver with blue eyes and long blonde hair. A very witty and sharp lady. She is a psychologist who works at a veteran's hospital with an emphasis on patients suffering from major depression and post-traumatic stress disorder. We first met at the VA, where I still work part-time in the pharmacy department. But I branched out and pursued my passion for teaching at the local pharmacy school. Jessica and I have been friends now for over fifteen years.

The main street of this beach town had one traffic light. Both sides of the main street were lined with souvenir shops, a diner, a coffee shop, several boutiques, a scuba and surfboard shop, bars, seafood restaurants, and a bookstore. The grocery stores were located on the outskirts of the town.

As we walked along the storefronts, Jessica wanted to explore the scuba shop and look into renting scuba gear. I was more interested in exploring the bookstore. We agreed to meet in two hours at the coffee shop and plan the week.

As we parted ways, I glanced at my watch. My goal for the next week was to get a good book or two and sit on the beach under an umbrella and walk the beach in search of sand dollars. I also wanted to enjoy some of the local fresh seafood.

I glanced at the shops along the way to the bookstore, looking at the diner's hours on the entrance glass door. As I walked past the diner, peering inside, the patrons sitting inside sipping coffee and eating their lunch stared right back at me.

A small police station with one police car parked at the curb was next to the diner.

An optical store came next. I stopped and glanced at the displays in the window and noticed the small waiting area was full of patrons sitting in their beach attire. Interesting! *I wonder if these beachgoers lost their glasses or contacts in the ocean.* It happened to a friend of mine while playing in the ocean waves with her children years ago.

I continued my stroll to the bookstore smelling seafood. I saw the huge sign, **Rare Collectibles and Best Seller Bookstore** in bold black letters, right above a flight of stairs down to the entrance door. I held on to the black painted steel handrail as I took the brick-lined stairs.

The worn wooden door had an open sign hanging on the other side of the door. Store Hours: 8:00 a.m. to 8:00 p.m. daily was posted. As I opened the door, a doorbell rang, ding, dong, ding.

I scanned around the bookstore, several patrons were looking at magazines, which lined the back wall in front of me, and some were looking at the books which lined the right wall entitled Best Sellers.

The middle rows were lined with books on each side entitled classics, mystery, romance, children's books, etc.

This is very well organized, considering the limited space, I thought. I slowly worked my way to my immediate right along the wall.

I scanned the books on the wall and was taken back. The books were carefully spaced so one could see the front cover. All the books were on the satanic occult. My heart started racing as I looked at the covers and titles of each book.

A plastic sign lay in between two books on the top shelf with black lettering on a white backdrop:

"Tattoos now available here with a picture featuring the tattoo of the month."

The picture of the "tattoo of the month" can be described as:

A forearm, which had a church with a Baphomet pendant as a steeple painted in black. A gray hand was wrapping around the wrist with a black ring on the index finger and long black fingernails.

"Can I help you?" asked a gentleman with black attire. He had black-groomed hair and a beard. Around his neck hung an inverted cross. His name badge pinned to his left chest said Tim.

I was so startled. "Uhm! You do tattoos here?" as I glanced at the tattoo on his right forearm, which was the exact tattoo featured as the tattoo of the month.

"Yes," Tim responded. "Let me show you."

Tim proceeded to take me past the cash register on the left directly at the entrance. We walked straight and then moved behind a purplish velvet curtain that completely covered this entrance from ceiling to floor.

I looked immediately to my left. I saw an office the size of a closet—just enough room for a desk, computer, and chair. The desk had stacks of paper on the far left near the back wall and sealed boxes neatly stacked high from the floor to the ceiling.

"Tight fit in your office," I said.

"It works for me as long as I unpack the shipments immediately," Tim responded.

The door on my right was marked "Restroom."

Roughly three yards in front of me was a gray door with a keypad lock. Tim put in the code and pulled the door open. He started the descent on the circular cement staircase. The walls were red brick.

At the bottom of the staircase, I looked up to find large windows right above the brick wall allowing an enormous amount of light in. Tim noticed I was glancing at the ceiling. A vibrant mural with reds, yellows, oranges, greens, and pinks encompassed the entire ceiling. Tim explained in detail who had painted it. It had faded over the years, but it was still breathtaking. Tim dove into how the tiles on the roof dated back to 1929. As Tim talked, I looked at the single silver table in the middle of the room with a hole in the center. A large drain could be seen under the table. I leaned up against the table as I noticed the table legs were mounted to the floor. Tim was still talking non-stop about this "historical" building, pointing at the mural and describing what seemed like each paint stroke.

He later noticed I was leaning on the table.

"Please, don't lean on the table. It is significant to our monthly meetings. We just had one last night. The first Wednesday of the month at 10:00 p.m., and on Halloween, we have a meeting."

"Here," Tim said, as he led me to a small round table against the back brick wall. It had two large notebooks with mostly satanic tattoos as he flipped through the plastic pages of pictures, "If you are interested. I use this Roll-A-Table as my workstation."

"Oh. Okay. Well, I appreciate it. I am going upstairs to find a good book to read on the beach. Thanks for the history lesson."

As I climbed the stairs, I glanced back at the brick circular wall.

2 Corinthians 11:14 kept coming in my mind: *"And no wonder, for Satan himself masquerades as an angel of light."*

I reached the top of the stairs with Tim close behind.

I went to the classic book section, then went over to the best-seller section. My spirit was so disturbed by what I saw downstairs. I couldn't concentrate. I grabbed the first book I saw, The Beach Cottage—A Novel. I paid and left.

I walked by the diner and texted Jessica. *Change in plans: I will meet you at 6:00 p.m. at the diner.*

Jessica texted back, *"Okay. Until then."*

Days passed. I continued to enjoy my beach umbrella, beach chair, book, the sea breeze, the seagulls flying overhead, beachgoers playing in the water, and my daily walks along the beach.

Jessica continued her daily long walks along the shore and multiple days of diving.

One morning, I arrived on the beach, and Jessica wasn't at our usual spot. Every morning, Jessica would wait for me wit a large cup of coffee and the beach chairs and umbrella ready for the day. The gentleman in charge of the beach equipment knew exactly what I needed as I waited. Once the beach chairs and umbrella were placed, I sat down and dug my toes into the cool sand. I opened my book where I had left off.

Twenty minutes later, Jessica arrived with two large cups of coffee in her hands and a newspaper under her arm.

"Nice hat," as I reached for my cup of coffee.

"I saw it and just loved it in one of the souvenir stores yesterday after my scuba diving. Sorry I'm late. I was reading the front page of the local newspaper."

Jessica sat down to my left in the empty beach chair. Looking at me, "Confession time," as Jessica took off her large brim hat and placed it on the sand.

"Thanks for the coffee. Okay. Confess," I said as I looked at her.

"I am talking about you confessing, not me. What happened on Thursday, the day you went to the bookstore? You have been acting weird ever since then. You don't talk as much as you usually do. Like you are in thought, constantly."

Only the waves crashing on the shore could be heard. Jessica continued as she opened the front page of the newspaper, *"Tourist reports unusual activity at the local bookstore."* She looked at me, knowing she got my attention. Jessica continued to read aloud, *"Tourist turns in snapshots from her phone to police revealing blood under the silver table and on the table legs."*

"Do I need to continue reading? You reported them. You know how I know? I saw you leave the bookstore and enter the police station. At the time, I was across the street at the scuba store. Not only that, well, confession on my part. Your sister told me to keep an eye on you, and she activated the share your location on your phone, so I could track your every move. You were at the police station for 1 hour and 25 minutes."

Raising my eyebrows, "What else did the article say?"

"Human sacrifices were being done monthly as satanic worship. Police never found proof for years because the clean-ups were so good until now," Jessica reads.

Jessica grabbed her coffee and large brim hat and said, "I'm going for a walk. Let's talk when I get back. Okay? I am interested in your thoughts."

"Okay," I said, sipping my coffee, "and I am interested in deactivating this share your location app you mentioned."

As Jessica walked along the beach, holding onto her large red brim hat and her top now blowing with the sea breeze, I glanced at the front page of the newspaper. I read the title of the article about the bookstore.

This article took up the entire front page and continued on a later page.

I put the newspaper down on Jessica's beach chair and watched the waves. Sipping on my coffee, I noticed a surfer running into the ocean with his surfboard.

My thoughts went back to what I saw at the bookstore. We should never dabble with evil spirits, which include horoscopes, tarot cards, mediums, trying to communicate with the dead, and Ouija boards. Our focus should be on the One who made the stars, the moon, and the tides. Seek the One true God who controls the universe. The pleasures and powers of this earthly world only lead to spiritual darkness.

"As surely as I live,' says the Lord, 'every knee will bow before me; every tongue will acknowledge God" (Rom. 14:11).

Anything that is not of the Lord is of the enemy. We must flee from such things. Even if it seems harmless at the moment, we must not give in to its temptations.

Never doubt that the powers of evil are alive and active in this world. Even when they are hidden like they were at the bookstore, they are there. The enemy likes to lurk in the shadows, ready to devour us when we least expect it: *"Be alert and of sober mind. Your enemy the devil prowls around like a roaring lion looking for someone to devour"* (1 Peter 5:8). Draw near to God at every moment of your life, and He will protect you from all forces of evil.

The Final Exam

I was walking up the hill at the University of Georgia campus on my way to take my required creative English final exam. The English building sat on a hill near the main library and the law school.

I climbed the stairs to the second floor of the English building to a small classroom. I bumped into David, who was my age—slender, fit, and sporting a military haircut. We met in English class and shared a political science class too.

As we walked into the classroom together, I asked David, "Are you ready for this final?"

"Well, creative writing isn't exactly my forte. I will be glad when this is over. Would you like to meet at the cafeteria afterward?" David asked.

"Yes," I replied as I sat at my desk.

I took my regular seat—the second desk on the first row closest to the door. As usual, David sat behind me. This classroom held twenty-five desks, but only nineteen students took this class.

Professor Baldwin walked into the classroom with his briefcase. He was in his mid-sixties, with gray, shoulder-length hair. He was slightly overweight, and had an enormous passion for teaching. He had a white shirt and brown pants on. His reading glasses were on top of his head. He opened his briefcase and took out two stacks of papers, and glanced at his sports watch.

The classroom was filling up. I had already placed my book bag under my desk. I put three pencils on my desk, waiting in anticipation for the final exam.

Professor Baldwin closed the classroom door and stood next to his desk with the stack of papers in his arms.

"Now, place everything away. There are seven essay questions. You must choose three—write two full pages, front and back, single space on any three essay questions. Notebook paper is provided at the back of the exam. You have three hours to complete the exam. Your grades will be posted in three days outside this classroom. Good luck!" Professor Baldwin stated.

Professor Baldwin went down each row, handing a copy of the final exam to each of us.

I glanced at page one of the exam:

Choose three from the following seven essay questions. Write two full pages—front and back—single space on each.

1. *Write your eulogy.*

2. *Why and how can we respect others?*

3. *During the COVID-19 pandemic, should first responders refuse to treat patients until appropriate personal protective equipment is supplied directly to them? Take a pro or con approach and support it. First responders are defined as medical professionals, police, fire department personnel, medics, emergency room staff, respiratory therapist, etc.*

4. *If you were able to change anything in the world, what would it be? How would you do it, and how would you finance the change?*

5. *What does love look like?*

6. *What would you like to be known for?*

7. *What makes a person good?*

I flipped to page two of the exam and saw a bonus question.

Extra credit points (10 points): Please, provide your thoughts for future essay questions.

I flipped through the remaining pages of the exam. It was all blank notebook paper.

I glanced at the first page of the exam and decided on three essay questions. I could hear David sigh heavily behind me.

Two hours had passed when I looked at my watch. I was making good time. I just completed two essay questions as well as the bonus question, and I was just starting on the third essay question.

Four students had already turned in their exams.

I was thinking, *"How is that possible?"*

"Thirty minutes left," Professor Baldwin stated and looked down again as he appeared to be grading papers.

"Time is up! Please, put your pencils down and place your exam at the end of my desk," said Professor Baldwin as he pointed to the left corner of his desk.

David had left as I gathered my things together. I placed my exam on Professor Baldwin's desk and proceeded to walk to the university canteen located closest to my apartment. Nicole, my twin sister, and David both texted; they would meet me there at 6:30 for dinner.

While I walked to the canteen, inhaling all the exhaust from the large university buses shuttling students across campus, I knew I got the bonus question right. The other three questions were debatable.

I found Nicole and David in the corner of the canteen. I placed my tray down with a plate of chicken, mashed potatoes, a roll, and a glass of water.

David looked frustrated.

"That bad, David?" I asked as I told him I got the bonus question right.

Finally, David perked up and said, "Let's hear it? I didn't get that far in the exam. I was not quite finished with essay question number three when the time was called."

"Okay! The bonus question," I said as I looked at Nicole and then David, "was to provide some thoughts for future essay questions."

1. What five things have you learned from life?
2. If you knew you had one year left to live, what changes would you make in your life?
3. God's speaking—what is He saying to you?
4. Is your character worth flaunting?

As dinner ended, we finished voicing our frustrations about the final exam and said our goodbyes. Nicole and I then walked home.

Exams were over for me, but Nicole had an organic chemistry final tomorrow.

I didn't want to disturb Nicole's studies. So, I got ready for bed. Once in bed, I thought about the millions of teachers and professors worldwide—their selfless pursuit of educating their students in order to help them excel.

"A teacher affects eternity: he can never tell where his influence stops."—Henry Adams

Jesus is our greatest teacher. More than anyone, He has affected eternity. In fact, He has promised eternity to all who proclaim His name. He has taught us what it means to walk through life as a follower of God, and He has done so by example. The power of His impact on the world flows throughout the Scriptures. His love is spread all over the world by those who continue His redemptive work.

"A good teacher is like a candle; it consumes itself to light the way for others."—Unknown

Jesus also was like a candle. He was consumed to light the way for others. He willingly went to His death on the cross to save us from our sins. Through His deed of amazing love and self-sacrifice, He has illuminated the way for all of us. All we must do is believe in Him.

A friend of mine, Janet, with such a sweet soul, stands only four-feet-ten with shoulder-length brown hair and always wears high heels. She retired from a long teaching career of teaching elementary school. She taught mostly English and social studies but loved teaching math too. Over her career, she took some students to the principal's office. It is not what you think. The principal of the school would be informed that the student would be escorted to the police station, which was located next door to the school, to report child abuse. The police would then contact child protective services.

Janet never knew what happened to any of the children she took to the police department, except one.

Two years ago, a teacher's aide noticed Janet's last name on her student list. She approached each child, inquiring if they were related to Janet, her former teacher. Sure enough, those two children are Janet's grandkids.

This teacher's aide was one of many students Janet took to the police department to report child abuse. This teacher's aide has the ability to intervene and report child abuse as well.

We will never know on this side of heaven the impact we will have in the lives of those we cross in life. Whether it be a smile, a hug, words of encouragement, or reporting child abuse, we need to make sure every moment counts.

"Recognize that every interaction you have is an opportunity to make a positive impact on others"—Shep Hyken

God has granted you the ability to impact others. It can be something as simple as a kind word or a small act of service. You never know what someone is going through and how much even the smallest act of kindness can change their day. We must keep our eyes open at all times to look for opportunities to serve others. God calls us to meet other people in their place of greatest need and provide whatever we can for them. When we do this, we please God.

Consider for a moment how many people you encounter throughout your day. Each one of those interactions is an opportunity to impact someone. God has poured His love out upon you, and you have a chance to share that love with others.

The Harvest

"Let us not become weary in doing good, for at the proper time, we will reap a harvest if we do not give up" (Gal. 6:9).

Dr. Sam was contacted by a former coworker and close friend, Dr. Kevin. Both men attended the same university in Ireland and later worked at an aerodynamic facility. Their careers spanned thirty-two years, and they both retired at around the same time.

Sam pursued traveling the world. Kevin, the more creative one of the two, pursued an idea of an amusement ride at an internationally-known theme park.

Kevin reached out to his friend and confidant, asking if he would be interested in evaluating and critiquing the ride before opening it to the public. Sam agreed. It would give them an opportunity to catch up. Sam was looking forward to the experience and reconnecting with his old friend.

At the amusement park, the two men greeted each other with a firm handshake and smiles. Kevin welcomed Sam to his new work environment.

"Quite different from our old workplace, that's for sure," Sam commented as he looked around at the entrance of the ride.

Kevin walked with Sam a few yards to a metal lectern with a bright light reflecting on the front.

"Welcome to the Harvest, Sam. I heard so much about you. I am Luke," Luke said as he came from behind the lectern to shake Sam's hand.

"Dr. Kevin," as Luke looked at him. "I have uploaded everything, and we are ready to begin."

"Okay. Dear chap. I want your honest feedback on this ride. We have had a few glitches, but I think and hope we worked them out," Kevin said as he led Sam to a two-seat Omnimover ride vehicle. "This vehicle will glide along a track and transport you through The Harvest. Enjoy!"

"Thanks," Sam said as he looked back and waved as the vehicle moved forward and around a bend into a dark room. The vehicle moved slightly to the left and very slowly forward as a giant screen appeared, showing a sizeable yellow cornfield scanning hundreds of acres. The wind caused the corn stacks to move. The sound of wind could be heard from a loudspeaker embedded in the vehicle's door. As the vehicle drove around a bend, the film projected a man in a large John Deere tractor plowing a large piece of open land. *Working the soil,* Sam thought.

Fertilizer was spread over the land using a large spreader. A scene of spring with flowers blooming as the sound of birds chirping over the loudspeaker played. Many men were seen walking down multiple rows with holes already made for the seed to be planted.

Sam noticed the vehicle was slowly going along a track that was going upward in a circular manner.

The film continued with rain falling and intermittent sun shining. The vast farmland footage showed a large storage unit made of steel seen in the distance.

Suddenly things went dark as Sam rode through a tunnel. He could hear flowing water in the distance. The Omnimover came to a stop as the lights came on. Luke stood next to the Omnirider, helped Sam out, and escorted him a few yards away to a log boat. Once on the boat, Luke waved Dr. Sam goodbye and said, "Enjoy the last leg of the journey."

Sam passed green vegetation on both sides of the boat as the sun's rays beamed through the windows overhead. Suddenly, the boat takes an unexpected dip down a steep decline.

The boat went along a bend, and Sam found himself in a greenhouse with vegetables and fruits on vines and above sprinklers turning on and off in certain areas. The boat came to a halt, and over the loudspeaker, a seven-minute summary of the benefits of homegrown vegetables and fruits and the benefits of a greenhouse.

The boat continued on to an open area with fresh fruit and vegetable stands on one side and a replica of a restaurant as a small villa on the other. The villa overlooked a field of crops as the backdrop. A substantial vegetarian menu was displayed at the entrance of the restaurant. The boat continued past a waterfall on the right and barrels full of seeds on the left. The aroma of citrus filled the air. The boat slowly came to a halt. Luke helped Dr. Sam from the boat and showed him to the exit. Dr. Kevin waited outside on a bench.

"Well, Sam. Your thoughts please?" Kevin said with a smile.

"I like it. That dip in the water ride portion took me by surprise," Sam said.

"We wanted to make it fun for the kids too. Let us grab dinner tonight. My treat," as the two men shook hands and said their goodbyes.

In the evening, Sam and Kevin met at their favorite restaurant. After the waiter took their orders,

Kevin asked Sam," What do you think of the ride?"

"Well done. I wouldn't change a thing. The ride did give me a great idea for a sermon."

"Sam! You haven't given up the Jesus stuff, have you? Come on. You are still teaching that weekly Bible study?

My word! What a fantasy world you live in," Kevin said as he looked at Sam and took a sip of his water.

"Hear me out, Kevin," Sam said as he looked into Kevin's eyes. There are many aspects of sowing and reaping."

Work the Soil (Plow)

In Matthew 9:37–38, Jesus says, *The harvest is plentiful, but the workers are few. Ask the LORD of the harvest, therefore, to send out workers into his harvest field."* God calls us all out to proclaim the gospel in different ways, but all of us are both sowing and reaping. God gives us all unique skills and passions. He utilizes these to continue Christ's redemptive work of proclaiming the gospel to the ends of the earth. Never forget, the whole world is the mission field!

Fertilizer

In our work of sowing and reaping, the fertilizer is God's Word. With its nourishment and godly wisdom, the Bible encourages people to grow. It provides the foundation necessary to become everything that God has intended for us to be. If we are to truly be powerful ministers of the Word and change lives for the gospel, everything we preach must be centered around the Bible. Within its pages is the truth of God.

Seeds

When we share God's Word, we plant little seeds of faith in others. When we cultivate those seeds by encouraging Bible reading and prayer, they bloom into beautiful plants full of vibrant life. Their growth is limitless and holds limitless potential. The bigger these seeds grow in the nurturing care of God, the closer they become to being mature believers in Christ.

Plants

In 1 Corinthians 3:6, Paul says, *"I planted the seed, Apollos watered it, but God has been making it grow."* Even though we are doing great work for the gospel, we must remember that it is only through the grace of God. We must never become prideful or take too much credit for ourselves. God is the author and sustainer of our lives. No matter how much we plant and water, at the end of the day, everything grows by the grace of God.

Greenhouse

The environment of the seeds is essential to their growth. We must surround ourselves with fellow believers and mentors. We must also be wary of how we spend our time. There are many deceptions of the enemy pervading our world that seeks to draw our attention away from the Lord. It is vital to stay diligent at all times and focus on activities that develop our faith.

Cling to the words found in 1 Peter 5:8: *"Be alert and of sober mind. Your enemy the devil prowls around like a roaring lion looking for someone to devour."*

Water

Water is essential to growth. Just as plants need consistent water to thrive, we need to return to God and the Bible for spiritual nourishment. In John 4:14, Jesus says, *"Whoever drinks the water I give them will never thirst. Indeed, the water I give them will become in them a spring of water welling up to eternal life."*

Harvest

Our work for the Lord is all about bringing as many hearts as possible back to God, so they can live throughout eternity in God's coming kingdom. In Matthew 18:12–14, Jesus tells the following story:

> *What do you think? If a man owns a hundred sheep, and one of them wanders away, will he not leave the ninety-nine on the hills and go to look for the one that wandered off? And if he finds it, truly I tell you, he is happier about that one sheep than about the ninety-nine that did not wander off. In the same way, your Father in heaven is not willing that any of these little ones should perish.*

God desires that everyone be in heaven with Him. He loves us all, and each person is irreplaceable to Him. This is why the harvest is so important. It is the very will of God.

Weeds

Weeds constitute anything in our lives that entangle us and limit our growth in the Lord. Sin is not of God, but of the world. We must be careful in discerning what comes from the Lord and what comes from the world.

Growth

The growth we have been discussing is all about maturing spiritually. We must grow in love. In Matthew 22:36–40, Jesus answers the question of what the greatest commandment in all of the Scriptures is:

> *Jesus replied: "Love the Lord your God with all your heart and with all your soul and with all your mind.' This is the first and greatest commandment. And the second is like it: 'Love your neighbor as yourself.' All the Law and the Prophets hang on these two commandments."*

Jesus is saying that a life pleasing to God is centered entirely around love! This makes complete sense because God Himself is the embodiment and very definition of love. So if we want to be ready for the harvest, we must grow in love.

Not only that, but we must also grow in mercy. Luke 6:36 states it clearly: *"Be merciful, just as your Father is merciful."* It's not a suggestion, but rather a commandment. God showed us the greatest of mercy in providing us with Jesus even while we were still sinners. Why, then, should we not show boundless mercy to others?

Growing in humility will help us accomplish this. Ephesians 4:2 reads, *"Be completely humble and gentle; be patient, bearing with one another in love."* There is no place for pride in the Christian life. Jesus walked throughout life in humbleness, gentleness, patience, and love. We are to emulate Jesus in everything.

Growing in all of these areas results in us growing in faith. Hebrews 11:1 says, *"Now faith is confidence in what we hope for and assurance about what we do not see."* Faith is all about trust.

For this to work within us, we must pull up all the weeds in our lives from their roots. No traces of them can remain. Anything that would hold us back from following Jesus completely is our enemy. Weeds have a way of taking hold of the good things in our lives and draining the life from them. In other words, clean the garden.

What is the best way to uproot these weeds in our lives? We must die to ourselves daily. Galatians 2:20

says, *"I have been crucified with Christ, and I no longer live, but Christ lives in me. The life I now live in the body, I live by faith in the Son of God, who loved me and gave himself for me."* This means that it's important to set aside our own selfish ambitions daily and instead choose to serve others and the Lord in everything we do. We must cast aside who we once were to accept who we are becoming in Christ.

The Parable of the Sower

In Matthew 13:1–8, Jesus tells this incredible parable which wraps up so much of what we've discussed:

That same day, Jesus went out of the house and sat by the lake. Such large crowds gathered around him that he got into a boat and sat in it while all the people stood on the shore. Then he told them many things in parables, saying: "A farmer went out to sow his seed. As he was scattering the seed, some fell along the path, and the birds came and ate it up. Some fell on rocky places, where it did not have much soil. It sprang up quickly because the soil was shallow. But when the sun came up, the plants were scorched, and they withered because they had no root. Other seeds fell among thorns, which grew up and choked the plants. Still, other

seed fell on good soil, where it produced a crop—a
hundred, sixty or thirty times what was sown."

Where have you planted seeds of faith in your life, and what has been the result?

"You see," Sam said, "this entire, beautiful experience that you've created with the Harvest ride directly relates to every aspect of the Christian life!"

Kevin sat silent for a moment, contemplating everything Sam had told him. Kevin had put so much time, energy, and work into this project. Through this conversation Kevin was starting to see the message of Christianity more clearly than ever before.

"I'd like to hear more," Kevin said, a bit shyly. "I'm sorry about my attitude before. That was rude of me."

"No problem," Sam said, smiling. "I'd be glad to talk more. I appreciate everything you've built here, and it's inspired me to share everything I've told you today. I've been praying for this opportunity, and I'm so glad to be here with you today."

The two talked for hours about everything they had experienced that day. Sam listened to Kevin explain all the work and the vision that went into his ride. Kevin listened to Sam eagerly explain the Scriptures to him. Kevin's eyes were opened like never before. The seeds within him were planted and being prepared for the harvest.

The Stolen

Cooper is the owner of the local café in Baldwin County, with a population of 19,000. The Friday lunch rush died down enough for Cooper to search his cellphone contacts. Brandon, a high school buddy of Cooper's, moved to the large metropolitan city of Atlanta one-and-a-half hours away.

Brandon pursued journalism after college and is the chief investigative reporter for an Atlanta newspaper. His first novel, *Murder in the Barn*, was a best seller last year. He is currently working on his second novel when he is not writing for the paper.

As the phone rang on the other end of his cellphone, Cooper greeted patrons walking into the café with a smile and a wave.

"Brandon. Cooper here. How are you? Did you finish your second novel yet?"

"Still in progress. How are Susan and the kids?" referring to Cooper's wife and their two sons.

"They are all well. Sales at the café grew 40 percent last year. So, we are doubling the size. We are adding a large covered back deck and an adjoining larger seating area."

"Wonderful! The back deck sounds great. It will back up to the large river. I remember when we went fishing over the summers and weekends during high school."

Cooper lowered his voice as he walked to his office, located just behind the long wooden counter. His wife was preparing a fresh pot of coffee.

"I may have something for you, Brandon. There is talk at the café," as Cooper closed his office door and sat at his desk. His voice turning to a normal pitch, "There is something going on at the south side of the lake."

"Like what?" with curiosity in Brandon's voice.

"Well, possibly human trafficking."

Brandon started laughing, "Cooper. In Baldwin County? You have got to be kidding me? Of all places, there? Why do you say that?"

"Some fishermen on a late run home saw a boat unloading 'something' into the abandoned cargo ship. You know the one docked on the shore for the last twenty to thirty years and deteriorating."

"Saw something? Could be drugs. Let me track down Tank and see if we can come this weekend and poke around. I will text you when I leave Atlanta. It may be tomorrow," as Brandon looked at his watch.

Tank was a good friend of Brandon and Cooper's from high school. They were like the three musketeers. After completing high school, Tank earned his nickname after twenty-two years of service as a Navy SEAL. After retiring from the military, he joined the DEA in Atlanta.

Two-and-a-half hours later, Tank and Brandon arrived at the café. The beauty of working as the lead investigative reporter at the Atlanta newspaper is that Brandon never had to be in the office as long as a story was submitted by 9:00 a.m. every Monday, Wednesday, and Friday.

At the café, Brandon, Cooper, and Tank caught up on the expansion details of the café. Sitting at a round table large enough to accommodate the three of them, they all enjoyed BLTs with chips and sweet teas.

Cooper swallowed the bite he had taken and looked at Brandon and then deep into Tank's eyes.

"Now. Changing the subject. The place you need to explore is two-and-a-half miles south of the Regent Bridge. The abandoned boat is on the southwest shoreline in a cove. The trees and bushes are so overgrown in that area it is easy to overlook, according to one of my customers," Cooper said.

Brandon took a sip of his iced tea, intently listening to Cooper.

"You can borrow my boat. It is in its regular slot at the pier. Here are the keys," as Cooper handed the boat keys to Tank.

"Sounds good. I know that general area from years ago fishing with my father," Tank said.

Brandon wiped his mouth with a napkin and asked Cooper how his father was doing.

"He is fine. Keeping himself busy with a five-mile run every morning and fishing. He misses Mom a lot," Cooper said, referring to the death of her mother two years ago. Both men were by his side at his mother's funeral.

The men finished lunch talking about their high school days and lectures they received from their parents when they came in late from fishing together.

Tank and Brandon drove in silence during the twenty-minute ride to the pier, passing their old high school along the way.

The Pursuit 250 twenty-five-foot boat sat in the last slot on the pier. Both men got on the boat. Tank sat behind the wheel as they cruised slowly from the pier. Their destination was roughly thirty-five minutes away.

The two men decided to leave Cooper's boat a quarter of a mile away and walk on foot to scale the area leading up to the abandoned boat. Daylight was slowly fading. They walked through the wooded area. They came upon the dirt road visible on Google maps of the area.

"Brandon. There are some heavy vehicles riding down this dirt road. Look at these tire tracks. Look at how wide they are," as Tank pointed to the tire tracks and took pictures with his phone camera.

They continue to walk down the dirt road with a large wooded area on both sides of the road. Suddenly Tank stopped and looked down the steep embankment.

"There she is," as Tank pointed to the abandoned boat. Brandon took a look in that direction.

"Brandon. Look over to the right. That appears to be a dirt path to the boat. See if you can find anything along that path. I will take this embankment and see if I come across anything," as Tank grabbed hold of a tree, slowly working his way down the embankment.

Brandon walked down the dirt patch to the shoreline. No trucks or boats were in the area. Birds were chirping above as the men met up at the steel bridge that led to the boat's opening.

Tank checked the steel bridge with his feet to make sure it was secure before walking across. Brandon looked at the water and exterior of this 1960s two-story houseboat. *It is not a cargo ship like Cooper was saying.*

Tank looked back at Brandon, "I'll check upstairs. Check this lower level, please."

Brandon nodded at Tank and said," Will do."

Brandon glanced at the ground all around him at anything that may look unusual. As he crossed the steel bridge, he looked on each side of the water. Nothing! Once inside the boat, Brandon found the floor to be very wet. *How odd. No recent rain,* he thought. Fresh footprints could be seen on the wet steel flooring on the lakeside entrance, not the landside. Brandon took his phone out and started taking snapshots with his phone camera. He needed to do the same with the truck tire markings on the way up to the dirt road. He glanced at the bow of the boat—all empty except for the one set of fresh footprints. Brandon slowly walked past the staircase Tank took upstairs. Walking beside the graffiti filled wall, Brandon found himself in the back of the boat with a sliding glass door opened to the elements. He noticed more footprints and took more pictures. In the corner to the left of the sliding glass door laid a gray elephant stuffed animal. Brandon reached in his back pocket and pulled out a large plastic bag. He carefully picked up the stuffed animal with the plastic bag without touching it and zipped it shut.

Brandon heard Tank coming down the stairs.

"Got something, Tank," as he showed him the plastic bag with the stuffed animal. "And I got a number of footprints. Anything upstairs?"

"Nothing but drug needles," Tank said.

"Let's go up the dirt road and take more pictures of the tire markings before it gets dark," Brandon said as he walked to the steel bridge. Tank followed.

After getting more photos of the tire markings, Brandon and Tank talk in-depth about their thoughts if there is "truly" anything illegal going on. They would have dinner at the café tonight.

The conversation continued over dinner. Cooper was filled in on the details. With full stomachs, Tank and Brandon said goodbye to Cooper and headed back to Atlanta. On the drive in the dark, Tank discusses with Brandon that he would talk with his agency to potentially set up a sting operation if his boss feels it is justifiable. The footprints, tire markings, and stuffed animal was a start.

Eighteen days later, Brandon receives a call from Tank. The conversation lasts two hours.

Brandon was taking notes nonstop on his notepad during their conversation.

"Tank. Give me time to pack a bag. I will meet you at the café as soon as I can," before hanging up the phone.

During the one-and-a-half-hour drive to Baldwin County, Brandon couldn't get out of his mind the findings. *Human trafficking in Baldwin County? Adrenochrome? What was that? That is why they needed children. Cooper's father, the ring leader! Did Cooper know?* Brandon's mind was running nonstop as he drove to the café.

Tears starting to roll down his face as thoughts of his own nephews came to mind. The thought of children being abused for money was disgusting, heartless, and unbelievable.

God's children being sold into slavery.

At the café, Tank, Cooper, and Brandon sat a corner table discussing the details of the case over coffee. Cooper was devastated over the news his father orchestrated the human trafficking operation. The fingerprints on the boat and Cooper's father's confession at the station would lead to life in prison. Cooper appreciated his friend's support during this difficult time.

Weeks had passed. Brandon was able to write multiple articles on illegal human trafficking and the adrenochrome market.

Cooper's father was sentenced to life in prison. He fortunately squealed on the many others involved in the operation, which led to the rescue of many children.

Tank was just grateful he could help uncover a despicable crime.

Cooper wondered what would have happened if he never spoke up about something potentially happening at the abandoned boat. With Brandon's and Tank's help, they were able to unravel the crime of the century in Baldwin County.

Untimely death, suffering, and torture endured by children, adolescents, and teenagers can be halted if people speak up and intervene. Unspeakable evil lurks in the hearts of many. The prayer and action of many can impact and transform the world, one human at a time.

"The only thing necessary for the triumph of evil for good men to do nothing."—Edmund Burke

> Rescue those being led away to death; hold back those staggering toward slaughter. If you say, "But we knew nothing about this," does not he who weighs the heart perceive it? Does not he who guards your life know it? Will he not repay everyone according to what they have done?
>
> Proverbs 24:11–12

We are ambassadors of Christ. This means that we must stand up for truth, righteousness, and love. We must not be mere bystanders as the world turns around us, but our calling is to speak up and be representatives of Christ in the world. This means that anytime someone is in need, hurting, or injustice prevails, we must stand tall on the truth and be the hands and feet of Christ in the world. God has called us to serve the needy, speak the truth, and be a witness for Christ in all the world.

Construction Site

Therefore, everyone who hears these words of mine and puts them into practice is like a wise man who built his house on the rock. The rain came down, the streams rose, and the winds blew and beat against that house; yet it did not fall because it had its foundation on the rock. But everyone who hears these words of mine and does not put them into practice is like a foolish man who built his house on sand. The rain came down, the streams rose, and the winds blew and beat against that house, and it fell with a great crash.

Matthew 7:24–27

Greg, a forty-seven-year-old day trader, hit it big recently. He sold a technology penny stock which sky-rocketed over the last three years. He is now a self-made multimillionaire—single, with no children, no debt, just enjoying life to the fullest. Greg is active in the local church, teaching Bible study every Sunday to an adult singles group and mentoring boys at the Boys and Girls Club twice weekly.

With millions of dollars in the bank now, Greg hired an architect to build his dream home. He found the perfect lot in a new, quaint neighborhood.

Greg spent a month going over the blueprints and making adjustments with the architect.

One afternoon, Greg drove to his vacant lot. Multiple trees needed to be removed in order to start building his dream home. His one-story home would soon be a reality. He was able to obtain a great contractor through his church, who he is meeting this afternoon.

As Greg was walking his lot, Jake, his contractor, arrived. Jake was highly sought after in this small town. He was known for excellent work, honesty, punctuality, and being a family and God-fearing man. In other words, Jake had integrity.

Greg went over the blueprints with Jake and could envision every inch of his new home.

Thoughts of multiple aspects of the house came across Greg's mind:

All the Boxes Needed

The packing from his current apartment to his new home would require many boxes. How many boxes would he need? But spiritually speaking, Greg would never box God in. Our Lord is limitless.

"*But Jesus looked at them and said, 'With man this is impossible, but with God all things are possible'*" (Matt. 19:26).

Many throughout the Scriptures doubted God's power and put Him in a box. Sarah laughed when God told her that she would finally have the child she had always wanted, even though she was barren. But God quickly proved to her that He wouldn't be confined in that box. Sarah became pregnant and bore a child. The disciples constantly questioned and doubted Jesus' power, but Jesus pulled through for them every time, blowing away any expectations that they had. He wouldn't stay put in the box they tried to put Him in.

We do the same thing all the time. We try to limit God's power. He promises us something, but we doubt, thinking it's just not possible. But as we learn in Matthew 19:26, all things are possible with God. He doesn't hold back good things from His children. He is all-powerful, and He uses that power to give those who believe in His name the things which will make them thrive. All we must do is trust in Him.

Electricity and Wiring

The wiring is needed in order to power the computer, phone, television, microwave, washer/dryer, and all the light fixtures. Who is your spiritual power source in life?

"I am going to send you what my Father has promised; but stay in the city until you have been clothed with the power from on high" (Luke 24:49).

We live in a society that's all about promoting self-sufficiency in everything. That's not what the Lord teaches. Yes, working hard is good and valuable, but we just can't do everything on our own. We need to rely on God. We need to admit with humble hearts that we need His help in our lives. Just as a child comes to seek their parents for help, so too do we need our Father in heaven.

When we do, He fills us with the Holy Spirit. The Spirit is our source of power for a life of holiness. The Holy Spirit guides us, leads us, and equips us for everything we need to do.

Water Supply and Plumbing

"Whoever believes in me, as Scripture has said, rivers of living water will flow from within them" (John 7:38).

Jesus is a constant flow of living water. When we draw from that water daily, we never thirst; hydrating us with spiritual purpose day in and day out.

Wood and Nails

"The thing that kept Christ on the cross was love, not the nail."— Billy Graham

Without Jesus' sacrifice on the cross, we would be lost.

The Pool

Dive daily into the Word of God and allow God's grace and mercy to flow over you.

God's Word, The Holy Bible, is an endless treasure trove of wisdom. Not only that, but Hebrews 4:12 tells us that *"the word of God is alive and active. Sharper than any double-edged sword, it penetrates even to dividing soul and spirit, joints and marrow; it judges the thoughts and attitudes of the heart."* God's truth is fresh and alive, speaking truth into the hearts of every believer. There is no substitute for daily time in God's Word.

Greg's thoughts were interrupted when Jake asked what timeline he was looking at in terms of completing the house?

Greg verbalized, "I'm not in a rush."

After forty-five minutes of discussion about the timeline and pouring over the blueprints, the two men walked the property, agreeing the construction would start in three days, weather permitting.

Four months went by, and the construction was complete. Greg's 1,800-square-foot home was done. The next project after moving in and unpacking would be to landscape the back yard. The front yard landscaping was completed by Jake's crew.

One day, Greg walked down his driveway to retrieve his mail. His neighbor, Joanne, saw him and walked across her freshly mowed grass to introduce herself. Joanne was in her mid-60s and athletic with gray hair tied back in a ponytail. Her hands were covered in dirt from the flowerbed she was replanting for the spring.

Greg saw Joanne almost every morning riding her bike past his home. Like clockwork, Joanne rode her bike at 7:00 a.m. as Greg turned on his computer to get the latest news and sip his coffee. Greg's office desk faced a large bay window overlooking his front yard. He had a clear view of the street and his bluebird box, which stood off to the right near the property line.

"I am Joanne. I moved in five months before you did."

Greg introduced himself, and the two spoke for fifteen minutes. Out of the blue, Joanne said, "You know, ever since you moved in, I have been getting this invitation from the church on Preston Road. Did you sign me up by chance?"

"No," as Greg smiled, "I go to the church on Stedman Parkway. I wouldn't sign you up for flyers. I would personally invite you to my church."

"Well, I am not interested in church. Never have been. It is all a bunch of fairy tales," she said as she was opening the church flyer and handing it to Greg. "I wish they would take me off their mailing list. It is a waste of money. By the way, nice job with the landscaping, Greg."

"Thanks," as they said their goodbyes. Greg proceeded along his walkway up one step to open his white front door with the church flyer in hand.

As Greg sat at his desk, looking outside the window, he opened the church flyer.

Large black bold lettering on top of the page was written:

Invitation

On the left side of the page was:	*On the right side of the page:*
A picture of rolled up cash	*A picture of an old rugged cross*
A picture of high-end luxurious handbags and two high-end cars with a backdrop of a huge mansion Gold, silver, rubies, and pearls were scattered under the mansion picture.	
The above items can be lost and will be left behind upon our passing. An appetite of the flesh will never be enough.	*Christ can provide an abundance of hope and inner peace. It can never be taken away*

At the bottom of the page was written:

Come join us at 9:00 a.m. or 11:00 a.m. every Sunday. We are located on Maple and Lemmon Avenue.

This Sunday, we will discuss:

- *Focusing on the material things of this world versus the spiritual.*
- *Being sold out to the pleasures of here and now versus the eternal.*
- *Turning away from the glitter and material things of this world and embracing a King you have never seen before.*

In our society today, we focus so much on forming a very specific self-identity. We are laser-focused on defining ourselves, going to great lengths to separate ourselves from the rest of the pack. Having a strong sense of identity is important and healthy, but we must be approaching it the right way. Ultimately, we belong to God: *"You are not your own; you were bought at a price"* (1 Cor. 6:20).

"There is nothing wrong with men possessing riches. The wrong comes when riches possess men."—Billy Graham

Everything we have is God's, and we are merely stewards of it. He gives us resources so that we would use them to help those in need. We must be careful to honestly evaluate how we use the things that God has blessed us with. Are we using them in ways that would please Him? That must be our ultimate goal.

As Greg put the flyer down, he looked out his window and thought of Joanne. What turned her away from the church?

Weeks passed.

Neighbors started gathering on the street in front of Greg's house one Monday morning. Greg was unaware of what was going on. It was 9:30 a.m. when he glanced at his watch. He pulled the curtain aside in front of his desk to get a better look. Police cars were in Joanne's driveway.

Greg quickly got dressed and went outside. Greg learned that Joanne was hit and killed while riding her bike. The suspect fled the scene and hasn't been found yet.

Thoughts of Joanne's death flooded Greg's mind for days. He never took the time to inquire about Joanne's family. Despite being neighbors for six months, Greg knew nothing about Joanne.

Struck with guilt, Greg couldn't say he was a good neighbor.

"Love your neighbor as yourself. There is no commandment greater than these." Mark 12:31 came to Greg's mind.

Multiple opportunities were wasted for sure. During Greg's recent retirement, he did nothing to get to know his neighbors.

Looking back, Greg was able to see an empty lot of land being transformed into a home he always wanted. Like the empty lot, let us be transformed into what God wants us to be and do.

"Faithful servants never retire...You can retire from your career, but you will never retire from serving God."—Rick Warren

There is never a point in our life when we should stop growing in faith, character, and love. God can bring transformation and renewal to you, even when you think you are far past that point.

Unaware

Spring had arrived, and things started to bloom as I glanced at the azaleas that lined the front of the house. I tapped on the screen door, waiting patiently for the famous former magician to answer the door. Magic Blake was his show name for forty years. He was a good-looking gentleman with olive skin, jet black hair, and a well-trimmed beard from a website picture I Googled. I found him through my journalism professor when I was drawing a blank on whom to interview for a writing project for my college class. This project would account for 20 percent of my final grade.

The solid wood door was opened by an elderly gentleman. He was well-groomed: he had gray hair, was cleanly shaven, was wearing a light blue buttoned-down shirt, khaki pants, and tennis shoes.

Through the screen door, I introduced myself. I told him he was referred to me by one of my professors at the local university. He commented that he was familiar with this professor despite having not seen him in ages. He said he wouldn't mind being interviewed and would certainly enjoy the company. The elderly gentleman opened the screen door and welcomed me in.

As I entered his house with a notebook and pen in hand, I scanned the living room. It was filled with furniture from the seventies. The sofa was cluttered with newspapers and magazines. The coffee table had a coffee mug, which appeared to contain old coffee. The walls were full of pictures and memorabilia from his forty-year magic career. The fireplace had only a grate and was very clean. The curtains were drawn closed, and it was quite warm in the house.

With an enormous amount of enthusiasm, Magic Blake explained in detail the various pictures on the wall, including the ones of his family. He apologized for his talkativeness, but he explained how he had been rather lonely since his career ended.

After talking through his career with the aid of the pictures on his wall, we sat on the sofa. He took out a deck of cards from a storage compartment built in the sofa and showed me various tricks. I was in awe. He then revealed "how" the tricks were done. An illusion for sure, I thought.

"Our perception of a magic trick is actually a deception," Magic Blake stated with a soft voice. "Just as Satan tries to do. If you believe in Satan, young lady," he added.

Magic Blake started quoting scripture at this point.

You belong to your father, the devil, and you want to carry out your father's desires. He was a murderer from the beginning, not holding to the truth, for there is no truth in him. When he lies, he speaks his native language, for he is a liar and the father of lies.

John 8:44

"And no wonder, for Satan himself masquerades as an angel of light" (2 Cor. 11:14).

"Be warned! From Satan's viewpoint, you are a pawn in his game of cosmic chess," —Adrian Rogers

"Prepare to be amazed," Magic Blake said as he got up from the sofa and led me to a large pillar, which was to the left of the fireplace.

Two large pillars reaching to the ceiling were located on each side of the fireplace. With a push of a button located on the left side of the pillar, which is unseen to anyone standing in front of it, a door opened.

"Illusions, like in the movies with camera tricks and stunts," he said as he pulled the door open.

"Wow!" I laughed, "Sitting on the sofa with you and looking around the room and even at the pillars, I would never have guessed this would open up."

"Let us explore. Shall we?" Magic Blake said as he lifted his right arm and swung it forward, pointing down toward the staircase.

Magic Blake flipped the light switch on the right wall before descending the steep, narrow staircase.

I followed closely behind, running my right hand along the brick wall.

As we reached the bottom of the staircase, I looked around to discover this was Magic Blake's secret chamber. Surrounded by white concrete walls, it was much cooler in temperature as compared to upstairs.

In the middle of the room was a steel table mounted to the floor. Magic Blake, leaning on the table, explained the number of hours spent practicing tricks and concocting new illusions.

On the back wall was a long wooden table that covered the entire length of the wall. It was littered with ropes, chains, and a saw.

I glanced at my watch and was surprised I had spent two hours with Magic Blake. I thanked him for his time and for sharing his secrets.

As we were about to climb the stairs, I noticed an open safe, large enough to hold a man.

I pointed to the safe and asked, "You must have used this in your shows too?"

He didn't respond as we climbed the stairs and then led me to the front door. I thanked him again.

"Young lady," as he looked at me, "let me leave you with a quote from Charles Swindoll, a well-known pastor in Texas. He once said the following:

Choose to view life through God's eyes. This will not be easy because it doesn't come naturally to us. We cannot do this on our own. We have to allow God to elevate our vantage point. Start by reading His Word, the Bible...Pray and ask God to transform your thinking. Let Him do what you cannot. Ask Him to give you an eternal, divine perspective.

He continued, "Put on the full armor of God young lady."

Walking down the walkway to my car, I thought about the safe. It didn't have a key lock but a code pad to have access. How did he manage to get out of the safe?

I stopped and looked towards the front porch.

In the car, I called my longtime friend, Nan, with excitement to tell her who I just spend several hours with.

Once Nan picked up her cellphone, I immediately told her the news.

There was a long pause at the other end.

Then Nan said, "Are you talking about the white house on the right side, going south on Hammond? Several blocks from the University stadium? That house?"

"Exactly," I said.

"Grace! Magic Blake moved in with his daughter in Wisconsin a year ago. The house hasn't been cleaned out yet, but has been sitting vacant for a year," Nan stated.

Disbelief in my voice, I said, "What are you saying?"

Nan quickly quoted Hebrews 13:2: *"Do not forget to show hospitality to strangers, for by so doing, some people have shown hospitality to angels without knowing it."*

"As a matter of fact, thinking back, Nan, he never introduced himself as Magic Blake!!"

Hospitality is a key trait in a righteous person. God calls us to love everyone as He has loved us. God holds nothing back in regards to His love, and neither should we. If we truly want to emulate Christ, we will be hospitable and welcoming to every we encounter in life. You never know who it is you are serving. As we read in Hebrews 13:2, some have even welcomed angels without even knowing it.

That reminds me of an incredible story from the Book of Genesis. First, a little context. Abraham is regarded as one of the holiest figures in the Bible. He has been revered and looked upon as an example of righteousness by many people of faith throughout the centuries. His faith was so great that the Lord chose Him to create a line of descendants that would become His chosen people, the nation of Israel.

Genesis 18 tells a fascinating story about Abraham. He and his wife Sarah are visited by three men. Being righteous people of faith, Abraham and Sarah were extremely hospitable to them. They shared a meal together and had a wonderful time centered around the Lord. Only later did Abraham realize that God Himself had visited him and Sarah. Could you have imagined if Abraham, thinking these were just three random men like anyone else, was not hospitable to them? He would have been turning away God Himself.

Always treat others with hospitality, respect, and love. In Matthew 25:40, Jesus says, *"Truly I tell you, whatever you did for one of the least of these brothers and sisters of mine, you did for me."* When we serve others, we serve Christ Himself. Never hesitate to meet the needs of others as you have the opportunity. God loves a servant's heart.

The Sacrifice

Deon is a creative design beautician at a high-end salon. At thirty-eight, he manages this world-renowned hair salon in Chicago. One year ago, he had his first heart attack. This event was a wake-up call, causing persistent shortness of breath.

Jenny, a retired accountant, was getting her haircut by Deon this rainy winter evening in January.

"How did you get started into cutting hair, Deon?" as Jenny looked at him and her wet hair in the mirror.

"Long story. I grew up with Christopher, my best friend in Brooklyn. Christopher's father, Bob, was our landlord. Christopher and I met in elementary school. We played baseball and basketball after school. You get the point. Fast forward to September 11, 2001. I went to see Bob, who lived in our building. He was crying uncontrollably. Bob was telling me that Christopher was on one of the planes that hit the Twin Towers. We cried together. Bob's wife died a few years earlier as well as his other son in an automobile accident. And now another tragedy struck. I decided then, and there I needed to serve my country. With Bob by my side, I enlisted in the Navy on September 15, 2001."

"During my tour of duty in Baghdad, my commander saw me shaving my head. He looked at me and said," Many of our men need haircuts. Set up a chair, sailor."

"Yes, sir. That is when my hair career started. I enjoyed cutting my fellow sailors' hair. I was actually good at it too."

Deon continued to shape Jenny's hair and started where he left off in the story.

"During my last tour of duty, I became injured. In being discharged from the military, I was undergoing treatment for PTSD and new-onset diabetes. I was asked what I was interested in pursuing career-wise because I was still able to work. The military would pay for any training needed. I chose hair school."

"In hair school, I learned there was a creative aspect of hair cutting for women. So, that is how I wound up here.

"Thanks for your service to our country, Deon. Whatever happened to Bob, Christopher's father?" Jenny asked.

"He died five years ago. He was a very accomplished man. Okay. I have some news? I was chosen as Director of Creative Design at the A Hair Academy in New York City. A hair stylist's dream come true."

"Congratulations! You will be missed. I hate to see you go," Jenny said as she looked at Deon in the mirror.

After Deon finished styling Jenny's hair and blow-drying it, she wished Deon all the best in his new career and health.

Jenny walked across the street to her car after paying. As she sat in her car, Jenny looked towards the salon's front window, thinking of Deon's sacrifice for our country. He is amongst thousands of men and women who have and still put their life on the line for our freedom.

Christ did the same. Not for the country, but for the world.

John 3:16 says, *"For God so loved the world that he gave his one and only Son, that whoever believes in him shall not perish but have eternal life."* God looked upon creation and saw a world in ruin and despair. Things had gotten to the point where there was nothing humanity could do to save themselves. They needed a savior. But who was up for the task? None but God Himself.

God became man, and Jesus was born to Joseph and Mary. The natural consequence of humanity's sin was death. So Jesus lived the perfect life that none of us could ever live, then served as our sacrifice on the cross. He paid the penalty for our sins after living the only blameless life ever lived. In doing so, He fulfilled all of the necessary requirements for humanity's salvation. He was the final and ultimate sacrificial lamb.

Not only that, but three days later, He rose from the grave. In doing so, He broke the power of sin and death. He shares that same power with every believer, granting us eternal life through faith. It's all because of Jesus and His incredible sacrifice for us.

Meditate on Christ's example and how you can live it out in your life. Celebrate all those who have sacrificed greatly for you, whether it be parents, other family, friends, or our armed forces. Let their illustrations of Christ's servant heart inspire you and how you live your life. Commit to meeting the needs of others before your own, and trust that God will provide for you every step of the way. Hebrews 13:16 says, *"Don't forget to do good and to share with those in need. These are the sacrifices that please God."*

The Plane Ride

Lilly and Maya got into their seats on the flight from West Palm Beach to Atlanta. Lilly is a sixty-four-year-old German woman; such a sweet soul, and she owns an art gallery with her husband. Maya met Lilly recently through a mutual friend.

Their carry-on was securely placed under the seat in front of them. Maya buckled her seat belt and glanced over at Lilly, who already struck up a conversation with her neighbor in the seat beside her. Lilly and Maya were in the same aisle, each having an aisle seat across from each other.

Maya closed her eyes as the plane was taxiing to the runway. She could hear Lilly still chatting with her newly-found neighbor. Maya's mind was racing with the many aspects of the flight and the plane itself.

The fuel: The tons of fuel needed to travel from one destination to another, especially when going overseas. Consider the fuel's weight, let alone luggage, food and drink carts, and passengers.

Fuel is needed to fly the plane just as God's Word—the Bible—is the fuel for our souls. Are you reading your Bible daily?

Luke 4:4 says, *"It is written, that man shall not live by bread alone, but by every word of God."*

There is no substitution for a daily Bible reading plan in the life of a believer. God has gifted us with the unlimited blessings of His Word so that He could guide us, teach us, and build a profound relationship with us. It's impossible to truly walk with Him unless you know what His Word says and you are striving to live it out daily.

The Bible is truly the fuel for our lives. Through it, God fills us to the brim with love, hope, and peace. Those things sustain us as we go throughout our days.

The airline mechanics: The mechanics make the necessary repairs and safety checks so we can travel safely. When it comes to repairing our lives, does our heart need to be repaired?

"The LORD is close to the brokenhearted and saves those who are crushed in spirit" (Ps. 34:18).

Our Lord is in the "heart transplant" business. He takes our old hearts of stone and replaces them with a new, healthy heart. God desires to draw us close to Him and bring us to a place of restoration. God longs to remind us that despite the pain found in the world, there is still reason to love, reason to hope, and reason to care.

The radar instrument is used by pilots and the flight tower for navigation just as the Holy Spirit for Christians. We trust pilots during fog, but not God? Why the doubts?

We tend to naturally have more faith in things of the world than we do in God when it should be the other way around. God created the world and everything in it. Why then would we not see God as in control and holding all authority over His creation?

We can rest assured that God is in full control of our lives.

The overhead storage compartment in planes that are used for carry-on luggage: My mother is notorious for having tons of baggage. She rarely travels light. Isn't it true that we usually carry lots of luggage in life—worry, guilt, jealously, shame, etc.? The list is endless. Christ intended for us to leave all our burdens at the foot of the cross.

"Cast your cares on the LORD and he will sustain you; he will never let the righteous be shaken" (Ps. 55:22).

Why then do we continue to carry around our baggage?

Please know that God wants to ease your burden. He is stronger than anything you will ever face, and He can take it from you. Give up everything that holds you back and give it into God's mighty hand.

Snacks and drinks on the flight: Pretzels or cookies? Choices? No different than the Bible. One man chose Christ, one rejected Him in Luke 23:39–43:

> One of the criminals who hung there hurled insults at him: "Aren't you the Messiah? Save yourself and us!" But the other criminal rebuked him. "Don't you fear God," he said, "since you are under the same sentence? We are punished justly, for we are getting what our deeds deserve. But this man has done nothing wrong." Then he said, "Jesus, remember me when you come into your kingdom." Jesus answered him, "Truly I tell you, today you will be with me in paradise."

Jesus offers us eternity, but we have the choice whether to accept it or not.

Maya started napping and didn't realize the plane landed until she was jerked forward in her seat.

Maya glanced at Lilly, who was still engaged with her neighbor in the middle seat. Maya then glanced out the window on her side of the plane and saw a number of men and women helping the pilot direct the plane to the gate with various hand signals.

After getting the luggage at the baggage claim, Lilly and Maya said their goodbyes. They would join up again in one week to return home. Lilly's friend was already waiting for her. Maya's former neighbor and her ride texted she was running a little late but would be coming shortly.

As Maya sat on the bench near the curb, she watched the people being picked up and dropped off. She ripped off her baggage claim ticket on her suitcase, which designated the flight number and the final destination. She rolled up the baggage claim ticket and got up to throw it away.

As Maya sat back down and looking around, inhaling all the exhaust from the cars coming and going, the thought of the Lord's desire for each of us came to mind. He wants to make our final destination heaven. Just like the criminal on the cross chose Jesus as his Savior, so can you.

Romans 10:9 says, *"If you declare with your mouth, 'Jesus is Lord,' and believe in your heart that God raised him from the dead, you will be saved."* All it takes to start an incredible journey with Jesus today is a genuine belief in His Lordship in both your heart and mind. This must be a belief that you are willing to profess openly. What will you choose?

Faith in the Father

Madeline descended the staircase as she gently held on to the wooden handrail. She could feel the soft carpet under her bare feet. Sandy, the family's one-year-old golden retriever, was at her side. She counted seven steps and sat down on the stair. She felt the warmth of the sun through the vibrant stain glass. Madeline closed her eyes and thought about the upcoming eye specialist appointment. She has seen six eye specialists already for her genetic defect impacting her eyesight.

Madeline just turned eight. Her eyes started failing a year ago. Sandy is the seeing-eye dog her parents adopted when Madeline's eyes began to blur. The family was residing in the United States at the time. Seven months ago, the family moved to Paris. The world-renowned eye physicians who specialize in Madeline's condition practice in Europe.

The family antique store, which showcases furniture and statues from the 1700–1800s, is thriving in Paris. The vibrant stained glass Madeline was sitting next to on the staircase came from a church in France dating back to 1798.

Madeline could hear Sandy panting next to her.

"Madeline," her mother, Marcella called.

"Yes, Mother," Madeline said as she stood up from the stair.

"I am going to the market. Your father is in the study. I will be home shortly. We will start our home studies after lunch." She heard her mother's heels on the kitchen floor. Madeline could hear the garage door opening.

In the distance, Madeline could hear her father talking on the phone. As Madeline descended the stairs, Sandy by her side, she slowly walked across the wood floor. She knew the number of steps before she reached the leather sofa on her left and the coffee table just three-and-a-half feet in front of the sofa. She made her way to the bookcase on the wall and started running her fingers across the leather-bound books—the wealth of knowledge each book held. Everything is such a blur. Reading is now impossible. She relied on audiobooks as well as listening to her mother read to her.

A braille teacher comes three times weekly. Madeline was picking up braille quickly, far exceeding her teacher's expectation.

Madeline's mother and braille teacher were incredible examples of Christ's love in her life. They served her in a powerful way, helping her to continue doing the things she wanted and needed to do, despite her worsening condition. They made her struggle more bearable and helping her to overcome these new barriers in her life.

Madeline found her way to the sofa. As she sat down, she felt Sandy's head on her feet. She turned on the audiobook, The Jungle Book.

Madeline could hear her father's footsteps...tap, tap, tap on the wooden living room floor.

"Madeline, I just got off the phone with Dr. Pierre. Our appointment is tomorrow at 1:00 p.m.," her father said as he sat next to his daughter on the sofa, kissing her forehead.

"Don't lose hope, sweetie" he said.

"I haven't, Father" she replied.

Never lose hope in God's plan. Jeremiah 29:11 says, *"For I know the plans I have for you," declares the LORD, "plans to prosper you and not to harm you, plans to give you hope and a future."* Even when it seems distant, never doubt that God has a plan for your life. He has created you for a purpose, and you can rest assured that He will see it through to fruition.

The next day, Dr. Pierre spent one hour and forty minutes examining Madeline's eyes. He reviewed her charts from prior experts and discussed in detail the only option he had for Madeline. The experimental eye surgery and implant had to be done quickly because of the rapid deterioration of Madeline's eyes.

Dr. Pierre had success with this procedure on three other patients with this same genetic defect, but all three patients were much older. Most of the eye loss was generally seen in the forty to fifty-year range, never this early. This case would be for the medical journals for sure.

The surgery will be performed in three days.

On the train ride home, Madeline's father held her hand and whispered in her ear, "Trust me. Everything will be fine."

Madeline squeezed her father's hand and said, "I know, Father," as she glanced outside the train window. Everything was so blurry.

Just as Madeline trusted her biological father that he sought out the best physicians for her medical condition, can't we trust our Heavenly Father too?

In Matthew 7:11, Jesus says, *"If you, then, though you are evil, know how to give good gifts to your children, how much more will your Father in heaven give good gifts to those who ask him!"* God always has your best interests at heart. He longs to bring you things in life that will help you to thrive in every way imaginable. God wants this because He loves you. We can trust that His intentions towards us are always good.

What is holding you back from trusting God?

"Trust in the Lord forever, for the Lord God is an everlasting rock" (Isa. 26:4).

After the eye surgery, Dr. Pierre wanted to see Madeline back in one week. He would then remove the bandages.

The entire week for Madeline was dark. Sandy guided her through the house. Her father and mother kept the faith that this surgery would give Madeline her complete vision back. *"For we walk by faith, not by sight"* (2 Cor. 5:7).

It may seem that we're often walking through complete darkness in our lives. It surrounds us on all sides, and we may have no idea where we are headed. As people of faith, we don't have to rely on sight. We have our faith, which illuminates every dark place because Jesus is the light.

The appointment day came for Madeline's eye bandages to be removed.

"Well, Madeline. Let us remove your bandages," as Dr. Pierre slowly pulled off the tape that secured the eye coverings.

Madeline's father stood on one side, while her mother on the other. Each parent was holding her hand.

"Please, keep your eyes closed until I tell you to open them, Madeline," Dr. Pierre said.

"Yes, doctor," Madeline said with a smile.

"Okay. Open your eyes, Madeline," Dr. Pierre said as he stared at the little girl with anticipation.

As Madeline opened her eyes, she looked at her doctor, her mother, her father, and all around the exam room.

"I can see, Mummy. I can see everything clearly."

Everyone burst out with excitement. Her mother hugged her daughter and husband.

The eye exam continued for another hour, and a follow-up appointment was made for two weeks.

On the train ride home, Madeline started crying.

Her mother, next to her, placed her hand on her back and leaned over to ask, "Why are you crying?"

"Mummy. Because we have to give Sandy back."

Her parents started laughing, and her mother said, "No, sweetie. Sandy is our dog. He is a family member. Just because you gained your eyesight doesn't mean we have to give him back. We will need to cancel the braille teacher, though."

Her mother looked over at her husband and noticed a tear roll down his cheek.

In closing: People say hindsight is always 20/20. True. But, we never know what our future holds. Corrie ten Boom said it best, *"Never be afraid to trust an unknown future to a known God."*

Looking back at our past helps us to learn from our previous mistakes. Through this practice, we can build character and grow deeper in our faith.

There are times in life when we will have to wait for a miracle. It doesn't always happen right away, but we must always trust in God's timing. He can see things that we cannot. In the meantime, seek out every opportunity to learn and grow in whatever trial you are facing.

The Abandoned Key and Lock Store

We live in the days of cyber security spanning from endless passwords, codes, badges, fingerprints, and iris scans. Likewise, security cameras and safes are available to secure and protect our valuables, ranging from financial data, gold pieces, guns, passports, paintings, medical research, and technology.

One day, I introduced Ruby, a good friend from a prior job, to Susan, a friend of a friend. Susan is from the Deep South. She owns a jewelry store, cuts, and designs her own jewelry. Susan explained each piece of jewelry she creates is one of a kind, just like opals. There are no two opals alike.

Ruby's family owns a lock and key shop, which has been sitting idle for years. Ruby's health has forced her into early retirement and the closure of the store. State-of-the-art security was installed upon completion of the construction of the store years ago and updated periodically. The store's property value has skyrocketed recently. This sits at a prime location on a busy four-way stop, just off a major highway. Susan heard about the property through me and wanted to take a look at it. She was looking at expanding her business and wanted to expand on prime real estate.

Ruby, Susan, and I approached the former lock and key shop one summer afternoon. The white concrete building sat vacant. Weeds were growing through the cracks in the parking lot. Newspapers and old flyers, plastic bottles, and soda cans littered the lot. None of the windows were boarded up. Ruby unlocked the glass door, which had been sprayed with graffiti. As we entered the building, we were hit by a wave of heat.

Ruby and Susan were chatting about the acreage of the property and the potential of salvaging the room-size vault located to the far left of where we stood. The two left to look at the vault.

I, on the other hand, wanted to explore the large room, which was on my immediate right.

Before entering the large room, I passed a large glass case. I changed my mind and decided I wanted to see the "safe room" too.   I could hear my tennis shoes squeak as I walked across the light tan vinyl flooring. I imagined the physical items Ruby must have stored in the vault over the years. It is quite different from what we store in our hearts.

If we unlocked what we secretly store in our hearts, what might we find?

Greed

"Remember one cannot serve two masters: God and money" (Matt. 6:24).

What we lock away in our hearts can be numerous: pride, racism, bitterness, hatred, jealousy, guilt, and on and on the list goes. When we allow these things to take root in our hearts, it affects our lives in every way. We are drawn further and further away from God, and our character is compromised. These things harden our hearts and make it hard to live life the way that God has called us to.

Only one key unlocks the safe full of guilt and bitterness: that key is forgiveness. God's mercy throws open the doors of our hearts. Once God cleanses our hearts, we are open to receiving the fruits of the Spirit instead. Once those fruits start blooming in our hearts, we have true treasures within ourselves.

One needs to be very careful about what takes root in our hearts. Pull the evil roots up and *"grow in grace, and in the knowledge of our Lord and Savior Jesus Christ"* (2 Peter 3:18). If roots of evil take hold of our heart, they will burrow deep down and consume us.

In Matthew 6:21, Jesus tells us, *"Where your treasure is, there your heart will be also."* We must be careful of the things we give our time to in life. If we give our time and energy to ungodly things, our hearts will turn away from God. But if we cling to things that are of the Lord, closer and closer to Him we will become.

Jealousy

The human heart has a natural inclination towards jealousy. We often find ourselves discontent, wanting things that are not ours. Paul shares with us invaluable inspiration on this topic in Philippians 4:11–13:

> I am not saying this because I am in need, for I have learned to be content whatever the circumstances. I know what it is to be in need, and I know what it is to have plenty. I have learned the secret of being content in any and every situation, whether well fed or hungry, whether living in plenty or in want. I can do all this through him who gives me strength.

God wants us to find contentment despite our circumstances because He has already given us everything we need. His love and providence will sustain us no matter what we face in life.

Resentment

The Bible is quite clear of its stance towards resentment and any other similar feeling: *"Get rid of all bitterness, rage, and anger, brawling, and slander, along with every form of malice"* (Eph. 4:31). These things have no place in the heart of a believer. God desires for you to give these things up to Him.

Ruby and Susan were now having a talk-a-thon about their husbands. So, I left to explore the other side of the building. When I came into the entrance of the large room, I noticed a large amount of natural light beaming through the windows. At this point, sweat was starting to roll down my back. It was so hot and muggy in here. A large glass case encompassed three of the four walls. All intact. There was enough walking space behind the glass case as well as cushioned mats for leg and foot support.

"You ready to go, lady?" Ruby said as she popped her head in.

"Yes," I said, looking forward to the air-conditioned car.

I heard Ruby and Susan chatting about negotiating a deal to sell the property to Susan and her husband. We continued to explore the property line around the premises so that Susan had a better feel of the property's magnitude.

After walking the property, we all agreed to grab lunch. It appears a good friendship was taking root between Ruby and Susan.

In closing, open the safe and release all the strongholds which are held in your heart. What you lock in your heart or safe will eventually be revealed. Just like a bottle thrown into the ocean with a note in it. Over time, the tides will bring it to shore and the note found. We use passwords to prevent entry into financial and personal information, but we leave our spirits vulnerable.

The Bible gives us this invaluable wisdom: *"For above all else, guard your heart, for everything you do flows from it"* (Prov. 4:23). God desires to aid you in guarding your heart. Allow love to take root in your heart, dispelling all sin from it.

The Ice Hotel

After checking with the receptionist at my internist office, I took a seat. I glanced at the magazines on the table to my left. Sports, travel, news, and medical magazines were nicely organized on the glass table. Most of the magazines were old, dated months ago. I grabbed the *Travel* magazine and scanned the cover for any interesting articles highlighted in this issue.

Ice hotel, page twenty-seven, caught my eye.

As I turned to page twenty-seven, I saw multiple pictures of the exterior and interior of ice hotels located throughout the world. The carvings and detail reflected in each picture were just unbelievable. Works of art were created from nature itself because each room and sculpture was made from snow and ice, including chandeliers reflecting multiple colors because of the lighting. One picture in the magazine reflected a hallway displaying ice sculptures of animals, plants, chairs, tables, and vases. The snow walls reflected trees, deer, beavers, and raccoons.

I scanned the waiting room and placed the open magazine on my lap. Just as the ice hotel is short-lived, so are our lives.

"What is your life? You are a mist that appears for a little while and then vanishes" (James 4:14).

Human nature makes it difficult to see anything outside of our own perspective. We are so wrapped up in our own lives that we don't often realize how fleeting each moment is against the backdrop of eternity. But God sees all, past, present, and future. We can trust Him to lead us in every aspect of our lives because He sees all and knows all.

As the ice hotel melts at the end of winter, God's *"word will never pass away"* (Luke 21:33) nor will His grace and mercy.

We can rest assured that even though our time here on earth is short, God has promised us eternity with Him. This helps give us perspective, as we know that we are working towards a much bigger and more significant purpose in this life.

The ice hotels are quite unique, with a different theme and ice sculptures every year. The intense amount of work and time put into the ice creation is something we need to apply in our own lives. As the ice melts and our lives pass away with time, only that which is sown for the eternal will live on.

My thoughts were suddenly interrupted as I was called back to get my vital signs checked before seeing the doctor. The visit helped me to realize how precious we are as God's creation. Just as the doctor seeks the best interests of my health, God wants the best for me in every aspect of my life. He is the great healer.

In closing, each ice hotel is unique and beautiful, just like each and every person God has created. God has placed His image upon every person living on the earth. They are all precious in His eyes. He wants you to see them the same way. Everyone is special, and you don't know what they are facing behind closed doors. Life is tough and everyone deserves grace. Leave it to God to judge. Rather, celebrate the things that make each person the unique creation of God that they are.

The Class Assignment

Mrs. Alma is a forty-seven-year-old woman married with two sons. She has taught at a private Christian school in Lafayette since her college graduation. This prestigious private school equips high school seniors to pursue and be accepted at such universities as Harvard, Princeton, and Dartmouth. Mrs. Alma teaches English to sixth graders all the way up to the senior class. She works 7:30 a.m.—5:30 p.m. every weekday, including one Saturday a month. She looks forward to having every summer off.

The small class sizes (up to eight students maximum) attracted her to apply in the first place.

This week's assignment was for each student to write a short fictional story and present it to the class. The assignment is limited to seven minutes and must tie in at least one Bible verse into the story. She assigned this to all her grade levels as homework. Each student would have two nights to complete the assignment.

Her sixth graders would go first. "Any volunteers?" Mrs. Alma asked her students.

Andrew stood up and walked to the front of the classroom. Andrew, with well-groomed blond hair, has a light blue button-down shirt on with dark blue khaki pants and a red, white, and blue bow tie.

Andrew glanced at his classmates and started with, "A man named Bill works at a large automobile assembly line. He is in charge of defects found during the assembly process, whether it be the nuts, bolts, hoses, car battery, or whatever it may be with the car. If a part is faulty, by production line rules, it has to be reported.

Bill was sitting in his small corner office, blinds open to the noisy assembly line. He peered in the large box full of car wheel bolts, which had multiple misaligned threads. Bill had an unusually high number of faulty wheel bolts this month than any other month this year. He would have to figure out why and write a report to the corporate office.

Just as those car wheel bolts have flaws, we have weaknesses. *"For all have sinned and fall short of the glory of God"* (Rom. 3:23). Our weaknesses show up in different ways. Some are drawn to anger, others greed, and others lying. But sin is sin, and we are all subject to it.

There is something faulty in each of us, something that needs to be fixed.

God is our master mechanic. His love and wisdom can penetrate even the darkest of sins in our lives. His power is greater than anything evil that lives within us. He can cast it out, bringing us to a place of restoration and wholeness once again."

Andrew walked over, placed his paper on Mrs. Alma's desk, and went back to his seat.

"Very good, Andrew," Mrs. Alma stated as she noticed Amy walking to the front of the classroom.

Amy is a very bright young girl whose father is the principal of this school. Her mother teaches Latin and Spanish, tennis, and coaches the track team at the public high school across town.

Reading from her paper, Amy said, "I have titled this 'Clubs.'"

"The history club requires one to pay for admission into museums and even the expense of international travels. The golf club requires one to purchase golf clubs, golf balls, and fees to play on multiple golf courses. The speech and debate clubs require travel to compete regionally and nationally. Wholesale retail memberships require a fee to join and an annual fee.

"Mrs. Alma," Amy said, as she looks at her teacher and then again at her paper: "My mother wanted to join the book club at the condominium high rise we live at.

Well, they required my Mom to write an essay in order to join. Now, the person who was going to evaluate the essay never mentioned her qualifications. My Mom just asked what language she should write the essay in since she is fluent in four languages. She never bothered to join the book club. She started her own club."

My point is this: Heaven is a gift. There is no fee.

"For it is by grace you have been saved, through faith— and this is not from yourselves, it is the gift of God" (Eph. 2:8).

There is no amount of money you can pay or no amount of work you can do to earn your way into heaven. It is a gift, plain and simple. God gives it freely to all who accept Jesus as their Lord and Savior. God's grace overpowers everything that would hold us back from entering heaven. We mustn't focus on perfection but rather on living a life that is pleasing to God. As long as you know Jesus, your salvation is secure.

"Very good, Amy," Mrs. Alma says as she takes Amy's paper from her stretched-out hand.

Jackie started her way to the front of the class as Amy sat at her desk.

"Class. This will probably be our last presenter for today. The students who haven't presented will do so tomorrow," as Mrs. Alma looks at Jackie and gives her a nod to proceed.

Jackie, with her brunette hair in a ponytail, is known by most as the daughter of the famous lawyer who has put numerous criminals in jail. Her mother, on the other hand, is the owner of a high-end car dealership in town.

"Voting," Jackie said, "is upon us, whether it be the presidential, congressional, senatorial, or the other local official races."

Her classmates look at each other at this point.

"At the age of eighteen, we can vote in the local and national elections. Some adults vote on just one issue like abortion or the economy. At school board meetings, our parents can vote to keep schools open all year round, for example."

Groans from her classmates could be heard.

"The school board can vote on how excess school funds should be used in the school system. When it comes to voting, we all have different views on different issues. But there is one thing we can agree on: Christ died for each one of us."

"But God demonstrates his own love for us in this: While we were still sinners, Christ died for us" (Rom. 5:8)

This common thread throughout all of our lives can build great unity between us. God's love knows no separation between people, no matter what else attempts to divide us. When we start to find distance building in our relationships because of differences between us, we must commit to focusing on the commonality of Christ between us instead. There is to be no division between brothers and sisters in Christ, no matter what the situation. Galatians 3:8 reminds us that *"There is neither Jew nor Gentile, neither slave nor free, nor is there male and female, for you are all one in Christ Jesus."*

"Thank you, Jackie," Mrs. Alma said.

"Oh, Mrs. Alma. I want to add that I'm running for class president and need everyone's vote. Thank you." Jackie placed her paper on Mrs. Alma's desk and sat down.

Laura walked to the front of the class. Laura is from a modest family. Her father is a private detective, and her mother a manager at the local diner.

Just then, the school bell rings.

"Laura, we will start with your presentation tomorrow," Mrs. Alma said as the students gather their books and head for the hallway to their next class.

Laura was all ready to present, but the delay was a blessing in disguise. Instead of being the last that day, she got to be first the next day. In Matthew 19:30, Jesus says, *"But many who are first will be last, and many who are last will be first."* The next day, she was able to leave the first impression upon her classmates with her presentation. She got to set the standard for everyone who was to follow. Her presentation was exalted above that of Jackie, who had a good message but ulterior motives in looking for the class' votes.

Those Dirty Words

As disagreements continue to flare in the political arena and voter recounts ensue, nature's beauty is showing her bright colors of orange, yellow, green, and red. Despite the beauty around us, many people choose to be engulfed and bombarded with negativity from the media. The profanity used by some broadcasters, celebrities, and the general public is shocking. Newly-painted graffiti can be seen on the side of buildings and bridges, mostly of those four-letter words.

God has gifted us with His creation. He meant it to be a vibrant, beautiful place abounding in hope, peace, and love. Instead, we have tainted it with hatred, strife, and profanity. We have blinded ourselves from God's presence in the world. But Romans 1:20 says, *"For since the creation of the world God's invisible qualities—his eternal power and divine nature have been clearly seen, being understood from what has been made, so that people are without excuse."* God's presence is evident in creation itself! We just need to open our eyes.

Instead of focusing on those four-letter words and using the Lord's name in vain, let us turn our attention to the four-letter words from the Bible that can inspire us.

Lord

The Lord is the author of the Bible, the creator of the world, and the source of our very lives. He is all-powerful. The very definition of love. We know God through the Holy Trinity, Father, Son, and Holy Spirit. Those three persons share the same essence, being one and three at the same time.

The Lord's presence is our greatest gift. He wants nothing more than to have a relationship with you.

Pray, Give, and Will

Rejoice always, pray without ceasing, give thanks in all circumstances; for this is the will of God in Christ Jesus for you (1 Thess. 5:16–18).

Because of Jesus' sacrificial work on the cross, we now have direct access to God through prayer. He wants you to come to Him daily with your deepest thoughts, hopes, and desires.

God wants to teach us to have giving hearts. God has given everything for you so that you might have salvation: *"For God so loved the world that he gave his one and only Son, that whoever believes in him shall not perish but have eternal life"* (John 3:16). If God was willing to give up what was most precious to Him, His very Son, in order to save you, what holds you back from having a giving heart yourself?

God's will is His plan for your life and the world that we live in. We can learn God's will through the Holy Bible.

Love versus hate. Which do you choose?

The Bible tells us that God is love (1 John 4:19). His character, His being, and His actions are the very personification of the word.

In his letter to the Romans, Paul reminds us that there is nothing in the world that can separate us from the all-consuming love of God. Romans 8:37-39 says:

> *No, in all these things we are more than conquerors through him who loved us. For I am convinced that neither death nor life, neither angels nor demons, neither the present nor the future, nor any powers, neither height nor depth, nor anything else in all creation, will be able to separate us from the love of God that is in Christ Jesus our LORD.*

Pure

In the famous beatitudes during the Sermon on the Mount, Jesus says, *"Blessed are the pure in heart: for they shall see God"* (Matt. 5:8). Anything in creation that stirs up anger, hatred, and strife is not of the Lord.

Lamb

Jesus is often referred to in the Bible as "the Lamb of God." But why is this? Why the symbolism of a lamb? To understand this, we must look back to the times in which Jesus lived. The people of Israel, God's chosen people, lived a life centered around temple worship. They would bring lambs to the temple to be sacrificed in place of them because of the sin in their lives. The innocent lamb being slain held powerful imagery that showed the consequence of sin in our lives. Jesus is called "the Lamb of God" because He was the final sacrifice for humanity's sin for all time. Those temple practices are over because Jesus was sacrificed for all of us.

Rest

In our world today, rest is hard to come by. Our schedules are filled to the brim, and we find little opportunity to relax. But rest is important. So important, in fact, that God has commanded all to keep the Sabbath, a day every week of complete rest. Do you take a Sabbath day every week? It is not just a suggestion, but a commandment from the Lord Himself.

Where are we to find rest in our hectic lives? In our relationship with Christ. In Matthew 11:28, Jesus says,

MICHELLE YOST & NICOLE YOST

"Come to me, all you who are weary and burdened, and I will give you rest." Jesus will carry our burdens, ease the weight on our hearts, and allow us opportunities to rest. No matter what it takes, reset your priorities, and clear a day on your schedule for rest.

Gift

We are blessed beyond measure by everything that God pours into our lives. He has given us the beautiful world in which we live. He has given us His Holy Word, the manual for our lives. He has given us the Holy Spirit to guide our lives and equip us for every good work. But the greatest gift God has given us is His Son, Jesus Christ. He is the source of our salvation.

"Every good and perfect gift is from above, coming down from the Father of the heavenly lights, who does not change like shifting shadows" (James 1:17).

The Bible is full of words we can hold on to during troubling times. But most of all, hold on to hope.

The Wood Shed

One Saturday morning, Joey was awoken by the newspaper delivery hitting the front door at 4:30 a.m. He had fallen asleep on the sofa once again. The pitter-patter of the rain on his roof would ruin his daily 6:00 a.m. run—three miles every morning, weather permitting. His doctor advised a fitness regimen and weight loss after his heart attack five years ago.

Joey is a 54-year-old computer design specialist. He is divorced with no children. He occupies his time with work, fitness, teaching Bible study to the youth group every Sunday at his church, and helping his father at the family farm on most weekends and holidays. His father has slowed down over the years, so Joey has helped more with the cattle and chickens. The family farm is a twenty-minute drive away.

Joey arose from the sofa to prepare breakfast and coffee. He would work some in the woodshed before heading to the farm. Joey spent the last three months after work building a new and much larger woodshed from the ground up to better organize and accommodate his tools.

Looking at his watch, Joey had two hours before leaving for the farm. Once in the woodshed, he opened the top box of the stack of four boxes full of tools. While unloading the top box, Joey started placing his tools on the large workbench and looked around at all the pegs on the walls, thinking where he would put what. As he looked at the tools, he thought of a great Bible study for the following Sunday.

The next day, his Bible study was complete: "Sowing Seeds." The following Sunday, Joey thought about discussing the various "tools" Satan uses to distance each one of us from God.

Joey thought he could talk about pride first. Pride led to Satan's downfall in the first place. He would then discuss the following list of ways Satan uses to destroy our relationship with God. Satan is the king of lies. He loves to tell us things like, "You don't need God. Why do you need Him?" or "The Bible is not true." He tries to distract us from what is important, like the Church and the Bible. Our obsessions have become with electronics, online video games, meeting deadlines...the list is endless...all of which consume our time. As we get further away from God, we suddenly become more consumed with doubt and discouragement.

Evil uses strife as another "tool" to divide us.

"Sin has many tools, but a lie is the handle which fits them all."—Oliver Wendell Holmes, Sr.

Joey got his thoughts back and started focusing on the task at hand, unpacking the boxes of tools. It just took one hour. All his tools were hanging on the pegs, and the boxes were broken down.

Joey's hands started to ache from unloading and moving the heavy workbench to the other side of the shed.

It just occurred to Joey he could add hands as "tools" to his Bible study lesson in his closing.

According to Billy Graham, just as an artist uses his hands to paint a masterpiece, "God has given us two hands, one to receive and the other to give with."

Jesus used His hands as a carpenter. *"Has not my hand made all these things?"* (Acts 7:50).

The devil is hard at work. It can be seen worldwide. Many individuals have left the church. Strife is in the home and workplace. We have allowed sin to be swept under the rug in the church and other institutions.

How?

We have allowed the devil in. In closing: As the hammer pounded the nails to hang Jesus to the cross, Jesus' death and resurrection have allowed us to be set free of our sins. Through God's love and power, we can cast out all of Satan's influence in our lives. When we do, God's love will shine through us.

The World that Serves Self

Rachel and I went to the park with Duke, my two-year-old dachshund rescue. Rachel has been a long-time friend of mine. The park consisted of clean cement paths with plenty of grass for the protected turtles that roamed this area. Iguanas could be seen climbing some of the palm trees.

A large wood dock that stretched at least one or two blocks allowed people to fish. On occasion, manatees could be spotted in the water. Older people gathered on the benches to chat, and bikers parked their bikes on the dock to take in the boats passing by. Seagulls squawked as they flew overhead. A white heron stood on the dock railing. The ocean waves could be heard crashing on the shore below us. Storm clouds could be seen rolling in the distance.

Rachel and I sat on the wood bench with Duke sitting at my feet with his snout sniffing the air. We sat in silence, taking in our surroundings. I observed a woman in her forties standing and speaking to a woman on a bicycle who was looking out at the water. She wasn't even listening.

That's part of the problem in today's society—me and mine. Those types of people don't assist others; they walk away from folks in the store trying to reach for something, never thinking past themselves.

They are selfish, egocentric, and narcissistic. Whatever you want to call it, it is prevalent today.

Egocentric mothers push their children away with their behaviors; some cause their spouses to leave and destroy families. Narcissist individuals are oblivious to what is going on. They create strife, not harmony.

Charles Spurgeon once said: "The greatest enemy to human souls is the self-righteous spirit which makes men look to themselves for salvation." Sometimes we start to believe in the mindset that tells us that we know better than God. After all, we are the ones going through these experiences, right? Wrong. We will never have anything close to wisdom that surpasses God's. 1 Corinthians 1:25 tells us, *"For the foolishness of God is wiser than human wisdom, and the weakness of God is stronger than human strength."*

Philippians 2:3 states, *"Do nothing out of selfish ambition or vain conceit. Rather, in humility, value others above yourselves."*

"The person who plants selfishness, ignoring the needs of others—ignoring God!—harvests a crop of weeds. All he'll have to show for his life is weeds!"—Rick Warren

As we were leaving the dock, we heard a call for help in the distance. It was coming from the water. A teenager apparently fell off his jet ski without his life jacket, about 125 yards from the dock. The current was very strong at this point because of the storm brewing in the distance.

A former marine and lifeguard (as we found out later) jumped into the water and brought the teenager to shore as the fire department pulled up.

This selfless act of first responders and all those on the front line look outward and not inward. We don't have to look far during this COVID pandemic. The doctors, nurses, respiratory therapists, and other medical staff have put their lives on the line to provide life-saving measures for patients with this lethal virus.

Individuals who stock the shelves at the grocery store and all the clerks who bag our groceries for delivery during lockdowns need to be recognized for their selfless acts. We need to do the same: look outward, not inward.

I believe transformation happens within us when our direction is focused outward toward others. Matthew 20:28 says, *just as the Son of Man did not come to be*

served, but to serve, and to give his life as a ransom for many."
If Jesus Himself, the only one worthy of our worship, came to earth to serve others and not be served Himself, what excuse do we have to look inward and not outward? Jesus had a servant's heart, and it's that same mindset He wishes to instill in all of us.

Decision

Diana closed the Bridge app on her iPad with a bit of frustration. One wrong card move in Bridge can cost one the game. She knew because she was learning to play this challenging game. Diana enjoys it and truly desires to become better at it.

Four seconds can change your life. Ask Jim. He is currently in rehabilitation, trying to learn how to walk with a walker after multiple surgeries. He thought checking his texts while driving wasn't a big deal since he did it all the time. It changed his life and the life of the lady he hit head on. Barbara, the lady Jim hit, died on the scene. That four-second decision drastically changed Barbara's family too. Instantly, her husband was a widower and her children motherless.

One decision can change everything.

A biblical example is Lazarus and the rich man in Luke 16:19–31:

"There was a rich man who was dressed in purple and fine linen and lived in luxury every day. At his gate was laid a beggar named Lazarus, covered with sores and longing to eat what fell from the rich man's table. Even the dogs came and licked his sores."

"The time came when the beggar died, and the angels carried him to Abraham's side. The rich man also died and was buried. In Hades, where he was in torment, he looked up and saw Abraham far away, with Lazarus by his side. So he called to him, 'Father Abraham, have pity on me and send Lazarus to dip the tip of his finger in water and cool my tongue, because I am in agony in this fire.'

"But Abraham replied, 'Son, remember that in your lifetime you received your good things, while Lazarus received bad things, but now he is comforted here and you are in agony. And besides all this, between us and you a great chasm has been set in place so that those who want to go from here to you cannot, nor can anyone cross over from there to us.'

"He answered, 'Then I beg you, father, send Lazarus to my family, for I have five brothers. Let him warn them, so that they will not also come to this place of torment.'

"Abraham replied, 'They have Moses and the Prophets; let them listen to them.'

"No, father Abraham,' he said, 'but if someone from the dead goes to them, they will repent.'

"He said to him, 'If they do not listen to Moses and the Prophets, they will not be convinced even if someone rises from the dead.'"

The rich man and Lazarus made different decisions during their lifetime leading to different eternal destinies. Lazarus chose God over riches. He lived out a godly life in service to the Lord instead of a self-centered life. God rewarded Lazarus for His faithfulness. The rich man was punished for his short-sighted attitude towards life.

Who will you choose to be like: Lazarus or the rich man? We must evaluate what is most important to us in this life. In Matthew 6:21, Jesus tells us, *"For where your treasure is, there your heart will be also."* We must focus on priorities on things that are pleasing to the Lord. When we focus our time and energy on ungodly things, our hearts are turned away from purity and holiness. We become like the rich man, whose heart was so consumed by his riches –the pleasures of here and now.

In Mark 8:36, Jesus asks us a powerful question that we must ask ourselves now: *"What good is it for someone to gain the whole world, yet forfeit their soul?"* This one decision is not only important in determining the course of the rest of our life, but it will dictate our eternity.

But no matter where you find yourself in life, it is not too late to decide and choose Christ as your Lord and Savior. We may not know when we will die; however, we can be sure of where we will spend eternity. Don't neglect this choice in your life.

"But those who chose to reject God during their lifetime on earth will be separated from Him for eternity. This is not God's desire but man's own choice. God holds every man accountable for his rejection of Christ."—Billy Graham

God has given us the freedom to choose.

Never Abandoned

"My help comes from the LORD, the Maker of heaven and earth" (Ps. 121:2).

A little over one year ago, I lay in an ER bed with my sister by my side. Nicole, my twin, who is also a physician, got the call at 6:30 a.m. from my brain and spine surgeon, Dr. B. He was doing the work-up on my new onset of back pain and spasms. My other physician completely ignored my neuropathic symptoms (numbness under my left armpit and left breast). So, Nicole took matters into her own hands, which is what her led to Dr. B.

The 6:30 a.m. call went like this:

> **Dr. B:** "Your sister has multiple tumors in her lungs and a spine tumor."
> **Nicole:** "Where is the primary?"
> **Dr. B:** "I don't know. I want to admit her today and do a biopsy of her spine tumor."

As I lay on the bed in the ER, waiting to be taken back for my spine biopsy, I had so much inner peace. It didn't make sense, given my situation. In a time where hope shouldn't prevail, there it was in spades. Philippians 4:7 speaks to this feeling: *"The peace of God, which transcends all understanding, will guard your hearts and your minds in Christ Jesus."*

This peace I was feeling did transcend all understanding. At that moment, I had the choice to choose the faith that offered me this unmeasurable peace or fear. I decided on faith.

Fast forward to the present: For six to seven months, I received ten radiation treatments to my spine and multiple rounds of chemotherapy. I was admitted to the hospital several times, including the intensive care unit, for a week with an oxygen saturation of 52 percent (normal range is 95–100 percent). I experienced numbness from the waist down for several months and numerous side effects from chemotherapy, including pleural effusions (excess fluid around the space surrounding the lungs, which causes shortness of breath). I lost my hair, had chemo brain, and shingles. But through all this, I kept the faith. A future spine surgery is needed to realign and support my spine from the tumor and radiation treatments.

I was going through a physical trial while my mother and Nicole were emotionally troubled. Many people focus on the ill person and fail to acknowledge the caregivers who are bearing the emotional toll. Their struggle deserves recognition too. They give so much of themselves in the care of their loved one. My sister Nicole and our mother, their presence during these trials was priceless to me.

"Trials teach us what we are; they dig up the soil and let us see what we are made of."–Charles Spurgeon.

I describe this trial as walking through the valley, tirelessly climbing my way to the mountaintop. I thought I was nearing the peak, but I had so many setbacks (side effects from chemo, hospital admissions, and so on).

Nicole made a good point. She said, "Michelle, no one can climb Mount Kilimanjaro in one day. You have to set up multiple campsites along the way. That is what the campsites are—setbacks. It takes time."

Her point is true of anything that we go through in life. Life is a journey, not a walk around the block. But we are not on this journey alone. We have God on our side, who is the master navigator and greatest companion there is. His ultimate power and insight are essential on our path. Even when we are met with devastating setbacks, we must not give up. When our strength fails, we must rely on the power of God, who is always right by our side.

During this entire trying season of my life, the question, why never ran through my mind. The questions were *what* and *how*. What can I learn from this experience? How can I impact others with what I learn during this travail?

Every challenging experience that we go through in life is a learning opportunity. These tough times also provide us with an invaluable witness, speaking hope into the lives of people who are experiencing similar circumstances. God grants us the blessing of being able to share His love through even the darkest of times. Our stories can inspire others. You never know how your story can impact another's life.

According to Rick Warren, *"God intentionally allows us to go through painful experiences to equip you for ministry to others."* Don't forget that Rick Warren has experienced the death of a son through suicide. For him to go through something so excruciating and still be able to give wisdom to others through it is a testament to the healing power of God in our lives.

Trials not only help us to learn, but they present opportunities to grow in character. God gives us the strength to persevere and makes us stronger through our trials. Once He carries us to the other side, we have confidence in the assurance that there's nothing we can't conquer with God on our side.

Not only so, but we also glory in our sufferings, because we know that suffering produces perseverance; perseverance, character; and character, hope. And hope does not put us to shame, because God's love has been poured out into our hearts through the Holy Spirit, who has been given to us.

Romans 5:3–5

Never forget that there is nothing that is impossible for God to accomplish. No matter what you are going through, it is not bigger than the almighty power of our Lord.

"I can do all this through him who gives me strength" (Phil. 4:13). When you live with God's power in your life, nothing will be impossible for you. You can move mountains with your faith. You can truly change the world with the message of the gospel. You have a unique voice to use along the way. God has given you certain talents and experiences that help you express your mission of sharing the gospel in a profound way that only you are capable of.

One final question to ask during travails is, who? Who is there with us during a trial?

Just read this Bible verse in Genesis and see who shows up:

Joseph's master took him and put him in prison, the place where the king's prisoners were confined. But while Joseph was there in the prison, the LORD was with him; he showed him kindness and granted him favor in the eyes of the prison warden.

Genesis 39:20–21

Climbing up this mountain of untouched, rocky, and sandy terrain isn't easy. No one said trials were. We are to *live by faith and not by sight* (2 Cor. 5:7). As the wind blows and the sands shift, slips and multiple falls are all part of the upward journey to recovery. Keep trusting the One who still turns sand into pearls.

Having walked through the valley and climbed the rocky mountain terrain with multiple setbacks, the important thing is not to focus on the negative, but on what lies above on the mountaintop, for the view is amazing! God wants to pull you from your lowest low and bring you safely to the most powerful moments of your life. He has the power to do so. The Lord will take all of your doubts, fears, and insecurities and replace them with boldness and power in His name.

"So do not fear, for I am with you; do not be dismayed, for I am your God. I will strengthen you and help you; I will uphold you with my righteous right hand" (Isa. 41:10).

At the moment you are confronted with your greatest trial, you can choose faith or fear. Which do you choose?

Abandoned Vengeance

A thirty-four-year-old businessman, Scott, was married to a very prominent pediatric surgeon, Dr. Inge. They resided in the Northeastern part of the United States with their five-year-old son, Matthew.

One day, Inge's entire world was shattered with the tragic loss of her son and husband. Despite being sought after by multiple universities nationwide, Inge decided to take time off to grieve, reflect, and pursue some of her passions.

She sold her home in the Northeast and donated her furniture to those in need. The only thing she kept was her clothes, pictures of her family, and her car. She pursued her desire to climb Mount Kilimanjaro and Mount Denali.

After twelve months of time off, Inge moved to a metropolitan city in the Southeast. In just two years, she became chief of the pediatrics department at a prestigious university. She was also well respected by her coworkers. National and international universities sought Dr. Inge to give talks on the three surgical techniques she developed.

That was eight years ago.

Present Day:

At 1:00 a.m., Dr. Inge was called in on a pediatric trauma case. An eleven-year-old boy was shot three times—once in the right leg, another in the left arm and shoulder. Such gunshot cases were becoming rampant.

After five hours of surgery, Dr. Inge stepped out of the surgery suite, removing her mask and gloves in search of a family member of this eleven-year-old patient named Alex.

Alex's older brother, Bryan, was the only family member in the waiting room.

Dr. Inge introduced herself and said to Bryan, "Your brother is resting well in recovery. A nurse should be out shortly to take you back to see him. The police will probably have some questions for you."

Bryan, with a lot of frustration in his voice, said, "I spent the last three hours with the police officers. Thanks, Doc, for your efforts. Alex is the only family I have left."

As the two finished their conversation, Dr. Inge went to the single women's restroom and locked the door behind her. She wept uncontrollably for ten minutes. She was the only one in the surgery suite who noticed. The tattoo on Alex's right upper chest belonged to the gang that was responsible for her husband and son's tragic death.

As Dr. Inge washed her face with cold water, she reflected on what she committed to years ago: *Above all, I will serve the Lord—committed to the healthcare of all God's children that come through my surgery suite.*

As Dr. Inge left the hospital, the sun was starting to rise on this crisp morning. She reached into her jacket pocket to see who was calling her cellphone.

"Hi honey," Dr. Inge stated. Her husband of three years was on the other line, waiting for her to come home. Their one-year-old daughter could be heard in the background.

As she hung up her cellphone, she realized, if she hadn't forgiven the gang members for the death of her first husband and son, she wouldn't be able to enjoy the blessings and joy the Lord has given her now.

Just like Dr. Inge, let's learn from her situation and emulate her decision. If the past is holding you back, perhaps you need to release what has taken hold of you. Is it anger, jealousy, or bitterness? Perhaps forgiveness is in order and overdue.

"If God didn't forgive sinners, heaven would be empty." —Author unknown. What a powerful quote! God has

shown us great forgiveness, and He asks that we do the same for others, even when they don't deserve it. We didn't deserve Christ's forgiveness, and He gave it freely anyway. The beauty of God's love comes from His grace.

"Forgiveness is God's command."—Martin Luther. Here is another quote worthy of our attention. Forgiveness is not a suggestion, it is a direct command from God. There is no other way to live as a believer in Christ. One cannot follow God and hold grudges at the same time. The life of a Christian person is a life of freedom and love. There is no freedom and love when you are bound to the chains of regret and anger. Forgiveness sets you free.

Colossians 3:13 says, "Bear with each other and forgive one another if any of you has a grievance against someone. Forgive as the LORD forgave you."

Matthew 6:14–15 explains to us the seriousness that God has for forgiveness: "For if you forgive other people when they sin against you, your heavenly Father will also forgive you. But if you do not forgive others their sins, your Father will not forgive your sins." Take the words of the Bible seriously, for they are the Word of God. Meditate on this verse, and think of anyone you have yet to forgive. Ask God to give you the strength to make those steps towards forgiveness, whatever it takes.

Conclusion

My mother, Karin, is from a small town in Germany called Herne. She is an eighty-two-year-old blue-eyed blonde who moved to the United States in the 1960s. Several years ago, the two of us were walking down the main street in Herne, reminiscing. Each side of the main street has row after row of coffee shops, stores, and restaurants. The main street ends at the train station.

While walking arm and arm down the Main Street, hearing people chatting and watching people coming and going into the stores, we noticed a church that has been there for ages. It had a slightly new look. The front portion of the church had been converted to a storefront.

Why? Many Germans are no longer going to church, and this particular church had to downsize.

The church in the last days before the return of Christ is well described in 2 Timothy 3:1–5:

> *But mark this: There will be terrible times in the last days. People will be lovers of themselves, lovers of money, boastful, proud, abusive, disobedient to their parents, ungrateful, unholy, without love, unforgiving, slanderous, without self-control, brutal, not lovers of the good, treacherous, rash, conceited, lovers of pleasure rather than lovers of God- having a form of godliness but denying its power. Have nothing to do with such people.*

The church pews embody fewer and fewer people, while bars and nightclubs are crowded. This is the sad reality of the times in which we live. Most people would rather seek the fleeting pleasures of the world than the everlasting love of God. We must never succumb to these temptations.

Just as Noah was obedient in building the ark, we need to be obedient in strengthening our relationship with Christ...*"Seek ye first the kingdom of God"* (Matt. 6:33). Let this be your goal in absolutely everything you do. Each moment is an opportunity to learn more about and draw closer to Christ. When you seek the kingdom of God first, everything else falls into place.

The pews may be cold in some churches, but it the responsibility of Christians to share their faith. As believers, we are the body of Christ. If it weren't for the disciples stepping out of the boat, we wouldn't have the

Church. The disciples sacrificed everything and devoted the entirety of their life to establishing the church. We can't take their work for granted. It's important for us to love, cherish, and be active in the church.

What part are you playing? Are you living a life of devotion to God? Have you made the commitment to live out His purposes in your life? These are important questions. Take the time to honestly reflect on your answers, and make changes where changes are needed.

Are you embarrassed about what others may think?

Remember, many of the disciples died a gruesome death for what they believed in. The uncomfortableness you may feel in sharing the gospel pales in comparison to what all of the martyrs throughout the century have gone through. Not only that, but people around the world still die for their faith every day. Look to them as an example of being bold in your faith.

Lead by example.

Mark 16:15 says, *"He said to them, Go into all the world and preach the gospel to all creation."* It's God's hope that we would take the message of the gospel to the ends of the earth. God wants everyone from every nation and tongue to know what Jesus did for them. He wants them all to enter His glorious kingdom and live there with Him for all of time. You can be the catalyst that helps someone secure their eternal destiny.

In closing, during my trial of radiation, chemotherapy, and multiple surgeries for my metastatic cancer, I never asked, "Why me?" Instead, the focus should be, "Use me." I continue to live by this mindset to this very day. I want God to use all of my experiences, both good and bad, to strengthen my witness to the gospel.

My prayer is that God would fill you with the same mission and passion. I hope that the stories you have read in this book motivate you to live a life pleasing to God. Never doubt His love for you, and never forget that He has a purpose for your life, prepared especially for you. Utilize every gift that He has placed within you, and forge a new path forward as a witness to the gospel. Seek the kingdom of God first every day and in every way. Live your life for others, and walk proudly as a child of the almighty God. Never forget: God is a caring shepherd amidst His sheep on an open green pasture, who wants to grant you total victory over any challenges.

Citations

The Train Ride

https://www.azquotes.com/quote/912521

http://www.morefamousquotes.com/quotes/3135935-we-do-not-fail-to-enjoy-the-fruit-of-the.html

https://www.Pinterest.com/pin/37647346873543749/

Leaving the Past Behind

https://www.brainyquote.com/quotes/edmund_burke_377528

https://www.yourquote.in/sandeep-kashiwal-u21r/quotes?page=2&sort=

Feeling Abandoned

https://www.brainyquote.com/quotes/billy_graham_382921

https://quotefancy.com/quote/775967/Billy-Graham-Although-we-may-trust-God-s-promises-for-life-after-death-and-the-certainty

https://quotefancy.com/quote/865712/Max-Lucado-
God-never-promises-to-remove-us-from-our-
struggles-He-does-promise-however-to

Abandoned Character
https://brainyquote.com/quotes/thomas_paine_117868
https://www.brainyquote.com/quotes/
billy_graham_161989
https://quotefancy.com/quote/1528130/Adrian-Rogers

Abandoned Mercy
https://www.brainyquote.com/quotes/
Mark_twain_120156

The Final Exam
https://hyken.com/customer-relationships/
on-being-real/

Construction Site
https://www.quotemaster.org/
q262604be511bd4ada3a693e3009d77f0
https://www.brainyquote.com/quotes/
billy_graham_150664
https://www.brainyquote.com/quotes/
rick_warren_395107

Unaware

https://quotefancy.com/quote/1528099

Faith in Father

https://www.brainyquote.com/quotes/
corrie_ten_boom_381184
https://www.brainyquote.com/quotes/
Oliver_wendell_holmes_sr_118599

The World that Serves Self

https://www.brainyquote.com/quotes/
charles_spurgeon_181483
https://www.Pinterest.com/pin/372321094175883807/

Decisions

https://quotefancy.com/quote/776024/

Never Abandoned

https://www.brainyquote.com/quotes/
charles_spurgeon_165812
https://quotefancy.com/quote/899559/Rick_Warren